nF418209

CONGENITAL WINNERS

by

Francis Ojima

CONGENITAL WINNERS

UNLEASHING THE WINNER IN YOU

FRANCIS OJIMA

Copyright © 2021 by Francis Ojima

Unless otherwise indicated, all Scripture quotations are taken from the King James Version of the Bible.

To request permission, contact the author at francisojima@gmail.com

The author has emphasized some words in Scripture quotations in block type.

Front cover image: Jeremiah Moses.

Edited by: Ene Elizabeth Adeka

To Joy my beloved wife and to my lovely children; John, Jane and Jude whom I have received in a figure. You shall grow to discover Daddy loved you long before you got here.

Acknowledgements

I appreciate God Almighty who inspired this book and supplied the needed grace to write it. It would have been impossible without him.

Many thanks to my beloved wife Joy, for being the perfect help meet for me.

I am profoundly indebted to my Editor, Dr Okpe Peter Ochefu, whose painstaking scrutiny and meticulous editing was invaluable in the execution of this project.

I will also like to appreciate my parents Mr and Mrs Francis Ajodo for their love and sacrifice over the years. I love the man you raised me to be. God bless you immensely.

CONTENTS

Introduction

The word "Congenital" is derived from the Latin word *congenitus* which is a compound word made up of two Latin words; *con* which means "together" and *genitus* which means "beget". *Congenitus* literally translates to beget (born) together. It is clear from the foregoing that congenital refers to traits or characteristics that were present in an individual at birth.

In medical parlance, congenital is used to describe diseases that a baby is born with. For instance, *Tetralogy of Fallot* is known as a congenital heart disease because it is present in the patients at birth.

The term "Congenital Winners" therefore means winners from birth. The core sentiment emphasized by this coinage is that we all were born with the potential for perpetual winning. As born winners, failure runs contrary to God's expectation concerning us and therefore breaks his heart. It is the earnest desire of our Creator that we excel in all we do because he endowed us with what it takes to do just that at creation.

The fact that we were able to survive the arduous journey through the convoluted birth canal of our mothers which many babies were not lucky enough to survive, confirms the fact that the capacity to win is innate to us. The sooner you realized this truth, the sooner you will begin to live your dreams.

The purpose of this book is to convince you beyond every reasonable doubt that you are a congenital winner and arm you with time honoured principles which will ensure that your winning potential is maximized. As you imbibe the principles enumerated throughout this book, you will never stop winning in Jesus name. Amen.

Chapter 1.
THE DEFINITION OF A WINNER

"You were born to win, but to be a winner; you must plan to win, prepare to win and expect to win."

-Zig Ziglar

Beads of sweat broke from his face as he tilled the soil by the winepress while trying to avoid being seen by the sworn enemies of his people who had literally made life a living hell for them. The thought of losing the product of this hard labour to the Midianite marauders who took pleasure in invading their land, plundering their goods and carting away their valuables was more painful than the aches he felt in his arms and waist.

Was there really a God in heaven? Did he care about them? Why was there such a contrast between the plight of his people and the might of their God? The sword of the oppressors had forced his people to be restricted to dens and caves. Fear was their constant companion and misery the bed on which they lay.

Lost in the wilderness of despair and almost drowning in the sea of despondence, Gideon was startled to consciousness by the voice of an Angel.

"The Lord is with thee, thou mighty man of valour."

That call and the series of events that followed it was the game changer for Gideon and his people. Based on the revelation that the Lord was with him and he was a mighty man of valour, he went on to lead an historic military campaign that ultimately led to the liberation of his people and the restoration of peace and prosperity in their land.

While Gideon wallowed in self-pity as a result of the terrible fate that befell him and his people, God called Gideon's attention to the winner in him, which needed to be unleashed for the emancipation of his people.

In essence, God was telling Gideon, "You are a winner, do not settle for less, do not look elsewhere, you were provided with all you need to win and keep winning right from the day of your birth.

So my answer to the question, *who is a winner*? would be YOU! Yes, you are a congenital winner! Do you find it hard to believe? If I could only get you to believe that you are the definition of a winner, my goal in making you part of a generation of lifelong winners would have been 50% achieved.

My job in this chapter is to make it abundantly clear to you that you are the definition of a winner and because I am a winner, I am sure I will succeed in that quest. So are you ready? Let's go!

THE PURPOSE OF CREATION

Genesis 1:26 tells us,

> *"and God said let us create man in our own image, after our likeness and let them have dominion over the fish of the sea and over the fowl of the air and over the cattle and over all the earth and over every creeping thing that creepeth upon the earth."*

Genesis 1:25

That we were made in the image of God means we share the same physical appearance as God and that's evident in the fact that many times in Scriptures, God is depicted as having eyes, nose, mouth and hands. Besides sharing in His physical appearance, being made in the likeness of God affords us the divine opportunity to partake in His core attributes which include holiness, power, love and invincibility at creation.

If we never get to agree on any other thing, I bet you will agree with me that God is a winner. The surest one at that. He has never lost a fight and He never will. He actually breathed that invincible, constant winning nature into you when He made you. So, it is safe to say you are a congenital winner, meaning you were born a winner! This is more than evident in the creation account we earlier read. The very sentiment that followed the creation idea was "let them have dominion".

A world of unbeatable winners was at the core of God's heart when He nurtured the creation idea. The mention of dominion over fish of the sea, fowls of the air and cattle doesn't necessarily refer to a commanding rule over those animals but rather an exercise of dominion in the part of the universe they occupy. So, men exploring the winning nature in them have built submarines capable of navigating the depth of the sea in total defiance to its boisterous waves. Now that is dominion in the sea!

Men drawing on the incredible repository of wisdom resident in that winning nature have built aircrafts which defy the law of gravity –dominion in the air. Countless technological and architectural wonders in our part of the universe give credence to the fact that there is a portion of the winning nature of God at work in man. If it is true of any man, it is true of you because the One who made them, made you and if they were made like Him, you sure were made like Him. A winner you were created to be, a winner you will remain.

You are not a winner because you have experienced a couple of wins in your life, but you will win and keep winning for the rest of your life because you recognize and it has become an indelible part of your consciousness that you are a congenital winner!

WHY THEN DO WINNERS FAIL?

I guess by now you are having a hard time reconciling the revelation that you are a winner with the experiences of failure or losses in your life. Winners and failures don't seem to belong in the same sentence right? They are contradictory.

To answer the question above, I will have to draw a bit from my medical knowledge. I promise not to bore you with our scary jargons. Having assured you, let's take a trip down the long corridors of Medicine.

It is common knowledge that diseases are broadly divided into communicable and non-communicable diseases. Communicable diseases are those which are transmitted from one person to another like HIV and Hepatitis B/C. The non-communicable diseases like diabetes and hypertension are not transmitted from person to person but are multifactorial in origin.

Most times, there is an enabling environmental factor that allows a genetic predisposition to those illnesses to translate into disease. For instance, someone who has the genes which predispose to hypertension may not come down with clinical hypertension until he gets himself exposed to smoking, alcohol and excess salt intake.

Another example is folks with sickle cell anaemia. Even though they have the genes for sickle cells they are not necessarily always in crises. They suffer crises when they are subjected to conditions that favour the sickling of their red blood cells such as excessive stress, infections, extreme weather conditions and so on. So, if the environmental factors are taken care of, the number of crises a "sickler" suffers can be reduced significantly.

In like manner, a winner can experience failures if the environment he is in does not favour the expression of his winning nature. A winner will continue to win as long as he avoids factors which choke and repress the winner in him. The winning gene passed to us by God our Creator needs an enabling environment for its full manifestation. Your duty is to provide that environment and as you do so, the last failure you experienced will be the last you ever experience.

Gideon didn't suddenly become a mighty man of valour at the point the angel met him. He had been that all the while. Yet he suffered subjugation and unimaginable oppression as long as he was ignorant of who he was. The moment he was awakened to the consciousness that he was a winner, he bade the path of failure farewell and never lost another battle.

Do you now believe you are a winner? I bet you do! Having recognized that you are a winner by creation and winning is the purpose of your existence, you'll need help creating the perfect environment for the full expression of the winner in you. This is what we will discuss as we sail through the subsequent chapters of this book. Fasten your belt, and get ready as I take the seat of the Captain to sail you through to the land of perpetual winning!

Chapter 2
The Devotion Of A Winner

"Success can only come to you by courageous devotion to the task in front of you."

- C.V Raman

Many years ago, there lived a young shepherd boy by the name of David. Being the youngest of seven sons born to Jesse his father, David was saddled with the responsibility of tending his father's flock. Even though he was an incredibly skilled musician and handsome enough to catch the attention of just about any lady, he was content to spend his entire day navigating through the meadows with the numerous sheep which he so tenderly nourished and nurtured.

On a fateful day while David watched his beloved sheep grazing in the open field, he suddenly heard a frantic cry from one of the sheep. Propelled by an adrenaline surge, he hurriedly dashed in the direction of the bleating sheep determined to rescue it from its assailant at whatever cost. When the captured sheep came into proper view, David was greeted with a spine-chilling realization. The sheep had his neck right in between the jaws of a ferocious looking bear, whose terrible looking teeth were fast closing on the sheep before it was momentarily distracted by the darting motion of the shepherd. So gut-wrenching was the sight that David's first inclination was to flee for his life.

It however dawned on him that he had two options: either to escape for his life, thereby wishing the bear *bon appetit* and his precious sheep adieu, or put his life in harm's way and battle the bear for the deliverance of his sheep. Everything within him favoured the former option as that was the easy way out, but he knew that would amount to betraying the trust reposed in him by his father. He resolved to do all he could to rescue the sheep, or die trying.

Mustering all the courage his heart was capable of and with the only weapon in his possession, namely his shepherd staff, he dealt a heavy blow to the back of the bear which made it growl and let go of the sheep. Now dead furious, the bear turned in the direction of his challenger making some guttural sounds which bore some real ominous foreboding for the young man who had just interrupted his meal.

By this time, the young man knew without a shred of doubt that he had crossed the line, but at this point, there was no going back. He braced up for a fight while praying for divine intervention under his breath.

"The Lord is my shepherd I shall not....though I walk through the valley of the shadow of death, I will fear no evil; for thou art with me, the rod and thy staff they comfort me..."

In the twinkling of an eye, the bear had pounced on him, sinking its claws into his arms as he fell backwards. With his back on the ground, the bear made to bury his deadly teeth in the flesh of David's face when suddenly supernatural strength surged through him. As though possessing the strength of a dozen men, he lifted the bear from off his body and threw it away. The bear crashed to the ground with a heavy thud. No sooner had he landed than he sprang to his feet again and dashed towards David intent on tearing him to pieces.

As it opened its mouth wide attempting to rip David's flesh off, David got hold of his beard and pummelled the living day light out of the bear until it died. David fell to the ground fatigued, perspiring and hyperventilating, but relieved that he had saved the life of his precious sheep.

Another time he faced a much more ferocious foe when a lion came for one of his sheep. Once again, without the least consideration of his safety, he fought against the lion and killed it.

The experience and confidence garnered from singlehandedly slaying the bear and the lion under his belt made him confident to win again when he was confronted with the monstrous champion of the Philistines, Goliath. Goliath's size alone was sufficient to make a soldier scamper and hide in fear. David was absolutely convinced that God who granted him victory over those bestial enemies would give him victory over this gigantic *Homo sapiens*. True to his faith, no sooner had the fight begun than he had sunk a stone into the skull of the giant, which sent him crashing to the ground. In the next couple of seconds, he had the giant's head in his hand, sealing an historic victory for the Israelites and warming his way into the hearts of his countrymen.

Devotion is feeling strong or fervent affection for or dedication to someone/something. It goes without saying that nothing less than devotion would have compelled David to risk his life in order to save his sheep. If he was indifferent or laissez-faire in his attitude to the flock, he most definitely would have run for his life at the risk of losing the entire flock.

His devotion, however, made him dispel fear and confront the enemies thus providing the ideal environment for the expression of his innate winning capacity. This kept him on top of his game regardless of the enemy he faced. Without the element of devotion, the winning gene would have laid latent within him while he suffered recurrent defeat.

Just like David, you have the winning gene in you. It's been there all along, because you are a congenital winner. It was right there even when you suffered your worst defeat, all the while yearning to be ignited by the fire of your devotion and regretting that you seem so laid back, pessimistic and resigned to fate.

Rise up buddie! You were created for much more! Get fired up by intense devotion to your purpose and watch yourself transformed from a habitual loser to a consistent winner. However, if you choose to remain haphazard, passionless and vigourless in your approach to your work, you will certainly get swamped.

THE WINNER'S DEVOTION TO HIS GOD

Every true winner recognizes God as His source. The winning gene which emanated from God thrives best in association with God. As such, even though some men may appear to experience some victories in spite of their estrangement from God, no one can attain their full potential without association with God.

One may quickly quib, how about renowned scientists like Charles Darwin, Albert Einstein and Stephen Hawking who didn't necessarily believe in God but made remarkable achievements in their respective fields?

As we established in the previous chapter, everyone created by God received the winning gene. We are all congenital winners. So that congenital winning trait, exercised by a discerning mind and enabled by the providential graces of God bestowed on both the good and evil, is near infinite in its potential. The element of God introduced to man at creation makes it possible for him to achieve just about anything he sets out to achieve. Perhaps, the most compelling credence to that allusion is found in Genesis 11 where mortal men like you and me decided to build a tower which spanned from earth to heaven. Talk about impossibility!

God, however, came to see what they were doing and knowing that nothing would prevent them from achieving their dream so long as their efforts remained concerted, He disorganized them by confounding their languages. This singular act emphasized His sovereignty over the winning capacity in man. Yes, you can achieve a whole lot drawing on the repository of skills and potential in you, but you can only go as far as God allows you to. You will do a lot more when you have God on your side.

It is equally pertinent to recognize that there is temporal winning and eternal winning. The man who makes all the money in the world, publishes countless papers, makes ground breaking discoveries but fails to recognize and acknowledge God as His source and His enabler is at best a temporal winner but a colossal eternal loser.

Mark 8:36 asks a soul searching question, "What shall it profit a man if he gains the whole world and loses his own soul?"

Put another way it will be "What shall it profit a man if he wins all through life and loses in eternity?" It is akin to winning a local league and losing in the world cup.

Victory in eternity comes to the man who has possessed eternal life. What is eternal life?

John 17:3:

"And this is life eternal, that they may know you the only true God and Jesus Christ whom you have sent."

Do you want to be a winner in time and in eternity? Get acquainted with God through His Son Jesus Christ who, by the way, is the personification of all wisdom. You will never know another failure.

Are you ready? Call on Jesus right now. He is closer to you than you can imagine. Surrender control of your life to Him and you would have hooked yourself up with the Maker of perpetual winners both in life and in death.

THE WINNER'S DEVOTION TO PRAYER

The importance of prayer cannot be overemphasized. Prayer is actually an index that measures our devotion to God. You can't claim devotion or dedication to someone with whom you seldom communicate. So the more devoted to God we are, the more we commune with Him in prayers.

Prayer is an indispensable exercise in the life of every winner because it recruits the powers of the Almighty God into the circumstance of the individual, thus ensuring the latter's victory. Prayer invokes the supernatural realities of God into our situation. The man who prays cannot fail.

To emphasize the importance of prayer, Watchman Nee said "Our prayers lay the track down on which Gods power can come. Like a mighty locomotive, His power is irresistible but it cannot reach us without rails."

Do you get the point? You have the responsibility to build the rails on which God's mighty power will ride into your life through prayers. Prayer is the inflow channel of Gods incredible power into our lives and circumstances. To neglect to pray is to rob ourselves of all the power at God's disposal.

God's word says to call on Him in times of trouble and He will deliver you and you will glorify Him (Psalm 50:15). The day of trouble may be when you are confronted with an insurmountable mountain or when a deadline is staring you in the face and meeting it seems impossible, or when you are confronting a sworn enemy at your place of work, who won't rest until you lose your job, or when you are faced with a difficult course as a student. It doesn't really matter what the challenge may be, just call on the Lord. He will answer you and ensure you triumph over every challenge.

In 2 Corinthians 2:14 the Bible says, "Thanks be to God which ALWAYS causes us to TRIUMPH (win) in Christ." Do you see? When you invite God to fight your battles or oversee your undertakings, you are bound to win and keep winning!

Let's consider the life of David for a moment. He was no doubt a winner by all standards and we have seen that his successes were largely due to his devotion. Let's look a little more closely at his devotion to prayer, to validate the claim that prayer is crucial to the successes of every winner. .

In Psalm 55:17, David gave us an idea of his devotion to prayer when he said, "Evening and morning and at noon will I pray and cry aloud. He shall hear my voice."

David had a prayer altar, where he met with God in communion at least three times in a day. It didn't matter how busy he was. Whether as a shepherd boy tending the sheep of his father or as a King, superintending the affairs of an entire nation, he made out time to commune with God in prayers. No wonder, he kept on winning. Yes, he was a congenital winner, but he understood that his winning genes were activated by the presence of the Giver and there isn't a place where His (the Giver's) presence is more manifest than the place of prayer.

So intense was David's devotion to God that he likened his quest for God to the way the deer pants for water. Deer are known to have relatively fewer sweat glands than other animals, as such on a really hot day, they can be excessively thirsty. Since they are unable to adequately achieve heat exchange with their environment via perspiration due to their sparse sweat glands, they try to achieve that via hyperventilating which is why they pant until they find a source of cool water to quench their thirst and normalize their temperature.

For the deer, finding water on a really hot day is like a matter of life and death. It is therefore remarkable that David compared his thirst for God to the deer's thirst for water. In other words, communing with God for David was like a matter of life and death because he knew his victory depended heavily on it.

In 1 Samuel 23 we see a beautiful account which emphasizes the depth of David's devotion to prayer. News had reached him that the Philistines had attacked Keilah (a city in the lowlands of Judah), and were robbing the threshing floor. David, as you well know, was a man of war. He had won several battles before that time and had the reputation of killing the once thought indomitable philistine giant, Goliath. However, he wasn't going to presumptuously head into the battle without hearing from God. He knew he could only win the battle if God was with him. Therefore, it behoved him to find out if God would have him fight in that battle or not. He therefore, went to seek the face of God and God told him to go against the philistines stating that He would give him the victory.

When David informed his men that they had to head to Keilah to fight against the philistines, his men were reluctant because they weren't sure of their safety. David had to go back to God to ascertain that God was really asking them to wade into the conflict and save Keilah and again, God said to go. He mobilized his men, went for that battle and won a resounding victory.

While in Keilah, Saul who was the King of Israel at the time and a sworn enemy of David seeking to terminate his life at all cost, got wind of David's presence in Keilah and decided to capture him. Somehow, David became aware of Saul's planned onslaught. The logical thing to do was to simply take to his heels, but he wouldn't until he got a word from God. David went to God in prayer asking him if Saul was indeed coming after him and God answered in the affirmative. He went on to ask God if the people of Keilah would hand him over to Saul and again God said yes. Only then did David decide to flee from Keilah with his men.

Another profound testimony of the commitment of David to prayer is documented in 1 Samuel 30. David and his men returned to Ziklag after an official outing only to discover that the city had been burnt with fire. Devastation wouldn't do justice to the state they found themselves as they watched the deserted city and came to terms with the reality that all their valuables including their wives and children had been taken away. So great was their grief that they wept like babies even though they were seasoned warriors. David's men were so heartbroken they even considered stoning him. He, however, encouraged himself in the Lord and went to pray to God. He enquired of God if he could pursue after the intruders and if he would recover all they had lost. God told him to pursue after them, assuring him that he would recover all without fail. He mobilized his men and they braced up and ran after the Amalekites who carted away their valuables and, true to God's word, they caught them and recovered all they had lost. Over and over David was confronted with seemingly impossible circumstances but constantly triumphed because he always made recourse to God's intervention through prayers.

Our natural gift and talents may help afford us some limited victories in life, but to experience victory by all means, at all times and in every place, we must plug into Gods infinite power through prayer. If you are familiar with wrestling matches, you are probably aware there are some of them in which the parties fight in pairs.

You have two opponents fighting in the ring while their partners wait outside the ring ready to jump into the ring when they receive a hand shake from the one in the ring. Once any of the contenders in the ring gets tired or feels overpowered by his opponent, he immediately reaches out for his teammate to come to his rescue. Prayer is something similar to that. It's the believer's way of reaching out to God with a handshake for Him to come into the ring of your life and take over your battle. You can be sure when God fights for you; the outcome is bound to be flawless victory! O how fond He is of fighting for you!

He said:

"Be anxious for nothing but in everything by prayer and supplication, with thanksgiving, make your request known unto God"

-Philippians 4:6

Add ceaseless prayer to your warring paraphernalia and be on your way to becoming an invincible champion.

THE WINNER'S DEVOTION TO GOD'S WORD

It's wonderful to pray! As pertinent as prayer is, it wouldn't avail much if it isn't based on sound knowledge of God's word. Charles Spurgeon said, "When people ask me which is more important between praying and reading the bible, I ask them which is more important between breathing in and breathing out." As a matter of fact breathing in and breathing out are equally important for the sustenance of our lives. One without the other will end our lives in a hurry.

The way I see it, reading the bible and prayer are two sides of the same coin by which transactions are made in the market of grace. One cannot succeed without the other. You are not praying correctly unless you are praying scripturally and you are not studying the bible correctly unless you are studying it prayerfully.

A cursory glance at the Psalms would suffice to discover David's addiction to the word of God. His life was practically compassed and regimented by God's word. He saw God's word as the fountain from which he drew wisdom to tackle his challenges and he was sure God's word would keep him from failure.

The following scriptures emphasize his deep devotion to the word of God:

"I will delight myself in thy statutes, I will not forget thy word."

-Psalm 119:16

"Thou art my portion o Lord, I have said that I will keep thy word."

-Psalm 119:57

"How sweet are thy words unto my taste! Yea sweeter than honey to my mouth!"

-Psalm 119:103

"Thy word is a lamp unto my feet and a light to my path always."

-Psalm 119:105

"Thy word is very pure, therefore thy servant loves it."

-Psalm 119:140

"Mine eyes prevent the night watches, that I might meditate in thy word"

-Psalm 119:148

"I rejoice in thy word as one that findeth great spoil"

-Psalm 119:162

"The law of the Lord is perfect, converting the soul: the testimony of the Lord is sure making wise the simple. The statutes of the Lord are right rejoicing the heart: the commandment of the Lord is pure enlightening the eyes. The fear of the Lord is clean, enduring forever: the judgments of the Lord are true and righteous altogether.

More to be desired are they than gold, yea than much fine gold; sweeter also than honey and the honey comb. Moreover, by them is thy servant warned and in keeping of them, there is great reward."

-Psalm 19:7-11

These and several other portions of the Psalms show us how much David loved and cherished God's word. He esteemed God's word sweeter than honey. He saw it as his compass, his light and his defence mechanism. He knew one of the most vital secrets of winning in life is living by the manual of the source of life. He must have acquainted himself with Joshua 1:8 which said;

"This book of the law shall not depart out of thy mouth, but thou shalt meditate therein day and night, that thou mayest observe to do according to all that is written therein: for then thou shalt make thy way prosperous and then thou shalt have good success"

Wow! The secret of prosperity and good success in all of life's endeavours is falling and staying in love with God's word. His word has inherent powers to make you an unbeatable winner. There's no man who has lived by navigating the deep waters of life on the speed boat of God's word who has capsized. Rather, they all make it through as outstanding winners.

Enoch lived a life devoted to the practice of God's word and God considered him too good to pass through death which is supposed to be imperative for all humans. He was translated to heaven without dying. Abraham lived in devotion to God's word and became the richest man in his generation. Moses was totally dependent on God's word and he went from being the son of a slave to the national leader of the Jews who procured their independence from Egyptian slavery.

Solomon started out his life totally devoted to Gods word and he became the wisest and wealthiest man on earth. Devotion to God's word made Paul not just an outstanding lawyer, but the quintessential Apostle. You too can permanently remain on top of your game as you make the principles revealed in God's word your modus operandi.

THE WINNER'S DEVOTION TO HIS WORK

I'm sure you are familiar with the saying, "All work and no play makes Jack a dull boy". You should also know that all play and no work makes Jack a loser but much work and less play makes Jack a winner.

Lionel Messi and Cristiano Ronaldo are household names in the world of football, both having duopolized the best player of the year award for about a decade. Lionel Messi is largely considered to be the more gifted of the two as he effortlessly produces breathtaking masterpieces, game after game.

As at 2012, Lionel Messi had won the best player of the year 4 times while Cristiano Ronaldo had won it just once. Everyone thought it impossible for Ronaldo to ever catch up with Messi but Ronaldo recognized he too had the winning gene in him. He knew he is a congenital winner and was created for nothing less than the top so he made up his mind to work his way to the top.

He set his nose to the grind, determined to stop at nothing until he achieved his dream. Fast-forward to 2017, Ronaldo equalled Messi's all-time record of 5 ballond'ors. How did it happen?

Carlos Tevez who played with Ronaldo during his days at Manchester United gave some insight into the incredible work ethic of Ronaldo. He said:

Cristiano always stops in the gym after training: for him it's an obsession and being the best in everything, he always arrived at work early. When the training was set for 9 o'clock in the morning, I arrived at 8 o'clock and he was already there. Even if I arrived at 7:30, he was already there. I began to ask myself, how can I get rid of this guy? So one day I arrived at 6 but he was already there! Sleepy, but he was there" (1)

Wow! Can you even imagine for a second how someone with so much devotion to his work wouldn't be a high flyer? The glories he has won with his various clubs and country, not to mention his numerous individual awards, are sufficient proof that his hard work has paid off.

Patrice Evra is one other colleague of Ronaldo's who testified to his amazing devotion to his chosen career. He was famously known to have advised folks against honouring an invitation to a dinner from Ronaldo. Why? Simply because he once honoured an invitation to have a dinner at Ronaldo's place and it ended up becoming another training session. (2) The man more or less lived, breathed and dreamt football. It was his life's devotion and it has become his spring board to greatness.

You too can get to the zenith of your career by adding devotion to your core values. Yes, you are a congenital winner but without devotion to whatever you have chosen to undertake, success may seem elusive. Success is attracted to a devoted man as metal is to magnet. Fuel the fire of devotion in your life and your faculties will begin operating at a whole new level of efficiency and productiveness. Then, the winner in you will find uninterrupted expression.

CHAPTER 3
THE DISCERNMENT OF A WINNER

---

*"A wise man's heart discerns
both time and judgment."*

-Ecclesiastes 8:5b

Advantage in adversity, blessing in barriers.

Celebration in challenges, dominion in difficulties.

Emancipation in enslavement, friends in foes.

Greatness in garbage, harmony in hatred.

Inroads in imbroglios, jubilation in jeopardy.

Knowledge in knockouts, largesse in losses.

Molehill in mountains, novelty in nothing.

Opportunities in obstacles, possibilities in problems

Quintessence in queries, riches in rags.

Solution in suffering, triumph in tribulation.

Upgrade in undoing, victories in vulnerabilities.

Winners in wanderers, x-factor in xenophobia.

The ability to see the silver lining behind every cloud is the virtue that separates winners from the crowd

ADVANTAGE IN ADVERSITY

David was sent by his Father to deliver food to his brothers on the battle field. When he got there he met a fear-consumed, browbeaten and almost capitulating bunch of soldiers. The nonstop intimidation from the Philistine warrior who had challenged them to bring a man from their ranks to fight against him had reduced their brave hearts to jellyfish. At the risk of them going into national slavery should their chosen warrior lose the fight, they debated among themselves who was a match for the towering Philistine giant. Of course, none of the Israeli soldiers was a match for Goliath who was several feet above their heads in height and who had many years of flawless conquests under his belt.

David knew he was no match for that Philistine giant, being just a teenager at the time, and with practically no war experience. He however, saw the advantage which they had, which others were oblivious to. They had the name of the Lord of Host who is greater than any warrior and who decides the outcome of every fight. He is Jehovah Nissi. The Lord who fights for His own. David recalled that the name of the Lord is a strong tower into which the righteous runs and finds safety. So, he decided to go fight against Goliath, not in his name, his skill or his experience, but in the name of the Lord. He made bold to tell Goliath, "You come against me with spear and sword but I come against you in the name of the Lord, whom you have blasphemed..."

No sooner had the fight begun than Goliath sank to the ground. Just one stone off David's sling was all he needed to bring the giant down because when God is involved little is more than enough.

Do you know that your association with God is an advantage to be explored even in the direst adversity? It doesn't matter how bad things appear, if you call on the name of the Lord, you will surely win. God's word said he won't suffer you to be tempted more than you can bear but even in the midst of the trial, the test or adversity, he will make a way of escape for you. That way of escape is your advantage but it takes a discerning eye to see it.

Many folks fail to see the way out that God has made and they end up being consumed by their adversity. However, winners see the advantage. They see the provision God has made. They see things working together for their good and they see the hurdles as stepping stones to their destiny.

Do not shrink in fear or be dismayed because of adversities, observe with keen attention and you will discern the advantage you have right in that adversity. As you explore that advantage you will certainly win and keep winning because you are a congenital winner.

BLESSINGS RATHER THAN BARRIERS

When the Israelites were on the brink of entering their promised land, a twelve man delegation was sent to spy the land and bring back word to the nation as to the suitability of the land and their capability to possess the land. Whereas majority of the spies returned with negative report, emphasizing the hugeness of the occupants of the land and their smallness in comparison to those guys, the winners in the bunch–Joshua and Caleb – saw the blessings in the land.

They saw the beautiful gardens, luscious fruits, milk and honey that flowed in the land. More importantly, they saw their capability to displace the occupants and take possession of the land. It will interest you to know that of all the men who went to spy the land, only Joshua and Caleb eventually entered the land. All the others who had a loser mentality did not make it in. Seeing blessings where others see barriers will take you where naysayers can only reach in their dreams. Keep believing. Keep trusting. Keep winning!

CELEBRATION RATHER THAN CHALLENGES

Ben Carson is a household name among neurosurgeons. He popularized the field of neurosurgery through his book *Gifted Hands* and succeeded in making it the dream of many young medics. Before his retirement he was Head, Paediatric Neurosurgery Department in John Hopkins University. We now take for granted the separation of Siamese twins largely due to the discernment of Ben Carson.

Earlier in his career he was confronted with the challenge of separating a set of Siamese twins who had their heads attached together and shared some vital portions of their brains. (3) `

Of course, most neurosurgeons wouldn't even contemplate carrying out the operation because of the high risk of death of one or both of the twins. Ben Carson had zero precedence, no experience to draw from and an overwhelming number of challenges to overcome in order to give those babies a chance at living a normal life.

Whereas everyone else focused on the challenges, he saw the celebration that awaited them at the end of the tunnel. Rather than quit on those babies, he chose to navigate the tunnel, punctuated by long nights of studies, research, consultations and practice. Finally, he assembled a team of distinguished experts with whom he was able to accomplish the epoch separation of the Siamese twins. The look on the face of the parents when they heard that both babies survived was that of pure joy. Naturally, it made the headlines and shot Ben Carson to limelight. It all happened because he saw the eventual celebration where most people saw just challenges.

DOMINION RATHER THAN DIFFICULTIES

The history of the Jewish people is that of successive subjugation to enemy nations when they sinned against God, and also deliverance from bondage to their enemies when they turned to God in repentance. In one of their numerous periods of estrangement from God, they were oppressed by Jabin, the king of Canaan. The captain of Jabin's host was Sisera. So formidable was the army of Jabin that he had 900 chariots of iron. Those could easily pass for nuclear weapons at the time. For 20 long years, he oppressed and enslaved the Jewish people because they had no way of confronting his formidable military might.

Even though all the military warriors in Israel saw difficulties whenever they considered a fight for their freedom, a woman by the name of Deborah saw differently. She saw the dominion of the Jewish people over their oppressors and she instructed Barak who was the captain of the Jewish army at the time to rally his troops and go against the enemy. Of course, the lily-livered captain wouldn't go except she accompanied him to the battle. She agreed to follow him, upon which he gathered his troops, went against the enemy nation and secured a convincing victory for the Jews.

What do you see when others see difficulties? Do you see dominion? If you do, you are feeding the winning gene in you a diet that makes for optimum performance. Therefore you are bound to win all the time and everywhere if you see dominion where others see difficulties.

EMANCIPATION RATHER THAN ENSLAVEMENT

As at the mid-1800s, the darkness of slavery still prevailed in the United States of America, especially in the southern states whose economy was mainly driven by the sale of the produce from their cotton plantation, upon which black slaves were made to labour long and hard. Black slaves despaired of life as they were made to perform perilous labours under the most unfavourable conditions and subjected to severe abuse and torture to eradicate any iota of resistance in them.

In 1860, a man who saw the absurdity and inhumanity in enslaving fellow men simply because they were people of colour ran for the Presidency of the United States. He was totally antislavery in his philosophy, so much so that the southern states which were at the forefront of slavery and considered it a lifeline for their economy, decided to secede from the United State once Abraham Lincoln won the presidential election. The seceding states, which included Georgia, Louisiana, Alabama, Texas, Mississippi, Florida and South Carolina, formed the Confederate forces and fought against the Union forces in the American civil war while trying to become an independent state from the USA and perpetuate enslavement of blacks on which their economy thrived.

Abraham Lincoln, however, released the Emancipation Proclamation in the second year of the civil war which declared slaves in the region of the confederate states free and made enforcement of their liberty a goal of the war. The war eventually ended in 1865 when the troops of the rebelling Confederate states were subdued by the national (union) troops. Slavery was effectively abolished and about 3.5 million black slaves were emancipated. (4)

It was possible because one man saw emancipation where others saw enslavement and resolved to stop at nothing in his bid to achieve that lofty dream.

You too can make a difference as you learn to see things through a shade of optimism and possibility.

FRIENDS RATHER THAN FOES

The Amalekites in 1 Samuel 30 invaded the city of Ziklag in the absence of David and his men. When David and his men returned, they discovered all their valuables had been carted away and the city burnt. They wept inconsolably and the men even considered stoning David for bringing them to such an awful fate.

David, who was practically at his wits end asked God if he should pursue after the enemies and God said yes. Consequently, they set out to catch up with the enemies and reclaim their possessions which were taken away.

In the course of seeking those enemies, they found a sickly Egyptian who was apparently famished and almost passing out. Rather than pounce on him and unleash all the pent-up anger on him because he belonged to an enemy nation and could be part of those responsible for their woes, they fed him and gave him a drink, after which he was revived.

On interviewing him, David discovered he was a servant of one of the men who invaded and burnt down their city and was ready to take David to the hide out of his enemies on the condition that he won't be handed over to his master. David's alliance with this supposed foe led him to the hideout of those in possession of his wives, his men's wives and other valuables the enemy had carted away as spoils of war. They routed the feasting company and recovered all their valuables.

Some of the people you consider foes may in fact have the key to your breakthrough. Not everyone who is not on your side or within your clique should be considered an enemy. Even if they are proven enemies, Jesus teaches us to love our enemies and do good to them that hate us. The love shown to that Egyptian slave won him over to David's side. Even today, the power of love is still able to convert sworn enemies to avowed loyalists.

This is not in any way suggesting that you be careless, let down your guard and flaunt your vulnerabilities before people who are capable of hurting you. It is rather alluding to the ability to discern people who aren't necessarily on your side, do not share your worldview and are perhaps averse to you in many respects, but who nonetheless possess certain answers or qualities that you need to realize your dream. Courting and winning over such people is an attribute of winners.

GREATNESS WHERE OTHERS SEE GARBAGE

In many parts of the world, especially sub-Saharan Africa, waste management remains a major challenge. The ever increasing population in these regions and the dismal waste disposal systems makes littered streets and walkways a common sight which is partly responsible for the dismal health indices in the sub-region.

Lorna Rutto, a Kenyan entrepreneur decided to recycle plastic wastes and produce fencing posts from these recycled materials. Since the establishment of her company in 2009, she has produced thousands of those fencing posts which are in high demand in her country and significantly reduced the plastic waste littering her country. She has provided jobs for many individuals and has saved several acres of forest land and trees which would normally have provided timber for those fencing posts if not for her innovation, thus enhancing an eco-friendly environment. (5)

Others saw just garbage but the winner instinct in Rutto said, "I could make something great from all these plastic bottles on the streets". Her ability to see beyond the ordinary has enriched her and earned her the recognition of prestigious bodies like the Cartier Women's Initiative Award, who named her their laureate for Sub-Saharan Africa in 2011.

Greatness is resident in you, my friend. You are just an idea away from its manifestation. Think! Explore! Unleash the winning gene that has been in you from the day of your birth. The world earnestly awaits your manifestation. Do not waste God's investment upon your life. Open your eyes and see. The key to your greatness might just be buried in a heap of garbage.

Harmony instead of Hatred

If ever hatred could be justified it would perhaps be in the heart of a man like Nelson Mandela who together with his fellow black South Africans suffered intense persecution under the apartheid regime. The white regime discriminated, subjugated, and denied the blacks of resources which was rightfully theirs.

As a leading political figure and the voice of hope for his oppressed people, Mandela naturally felt the need to fight against white domination, seek equal rights and justice for the blacks who were being maltreated, and equitable distribution of resources between the white and black populations. His stand against the prejudicial polices of the apartheid regime eventually landed him in jail. The fight for the liberation of his people kept him in jail for 27 years. That period was enough for anyone to be neck-deep in hatred towards his persecutors, but not Mandela.

When he was released from prison he went ahead to become the first black president of South Africa which gave him ample opportunity to have his revenge on the white South Africans for all the sufferings they had put him and his fellow black country men through. He however, chose to forgive them and promoted harmonious coexistence of the white and black population. This earned him numerous honours including the Nobel Peace Prize in 1993. (6)

Winners see beyond the pettiness of hatred and revenge. Those negative emotions are ignoble and beneath the dignity of every true winner. God says, "Vengeance is mine, I will repay." So rather than seek revenge, learn to forgive and let go of the hurtful feelings and God will promote you.

INROAD RATHER THAN IMBROGLIO

The Jewish people were made to suffer severe torture and untold hardship as slaves to the Egyptians. This bitter ordeal lasted over 400 years. At the height of their pain, the Hebrews cried to God for help and he sent Moses to deliver them from Egyptian bondage.

Moses approached the then Pharaoh to request release of his people but met a brick wall. Pharaoh adamantly refused his appeal and rendered any hope for release entertained by the Jewish people a mirage, or so he thought.

The negotiations went back and forth for a while, and still Pharaoh's position was an emphatic no! Eventually, Moses resorted to demonstrate spiritual might assuming that would compel Pharaoh to give in to their demands. Moses performed series of supernatural acts but Pharaoh's magicians kept replicating them until they saw the unmatched irreproducible power of the Most High God turning dust to lice, causing an epidemic of boils and even slaying all the first born sons of the Egyptians. This eventually led to the release of the Jewish people from slavery to the Egyptians.

If Moses had given up when confronted by the imbroglio in his initial negotiations with Pharaoh, his people would have remained slaves to the Egyptians. However, the winning spirit in him made him to see an inroad to their eventual liberation, in spite of the obstruction produced by Pharaoh's obstinacy. He won because he saw an inroad where others saw an impassable imbroglio.

Winners never give up! They keep believing! When you have God on your side, there is no mountain that is insurmountable. You will ride right through the mountain if need be to your victory as Moses did.

JUBILATION RATHER THAN JEOPARDY

In 1 Chronicles 20, we read of an interesting account of a combined military attack on the Israelites. The armies of the Moabites, Ammonites and other allied forces decided to wage war against the Jews. So huge was their assailants that the nation of Israel under the leadership of Hezekiah was thrown into panic mode due to the perceived jeopardy.

Then came the winner man who saw beyond the apparent jeopardy. He was Jahaziel. He had the Spirit of God; the ever winning Spirit. He stilled the people and reassured them that they need not panic as they were not going to fight in that battle because the Lord had made the battle his own. He assured them that the Lord was with them, they therefore had no reason to fear.

Hezekiah, the King eventually got fired up by the reassuring words of Jahaziel and braced up to face his enemies with the most unusual military strategy ever known to man. They appointed singers and instrumentalists to praise the name of the Lord and the beauty of His holiness, and while they were singing and jubilating, the Lord sent an ambush against their enemies and they were all destroyed. Victory came to the Jews in this instant because someone saw beyond the jeopardy that loomed. He saw jubilation at the end of the tunnel. He stirred the heart of the people to celebrate the might of their God rather than succumb to the weight of their fears and God came through for them.

That's the winning mentality. It doesn't back down. It doesn't make excuses. It is hopeful, optimistic and incorrigibly insistent on victory.

KNOWLEDGE RATHER THAN KNOCKOUTS

Anthony Joshua was the almost undisputed champion of the heavy weight division of the world boxing federation. Having claimed 4 of the 5 belts available for grabs in the division, he reigned supreme.

When Andy Ruiz, the rather chubby Mexican boxer, was pitted against him in a challenge for the world title, everyone thought Joshua would technically knock out Ruiz in his characteristic way. Imagine everyone's shock when Ruiz not only won Joshua but knocked him out severally before finally giving him a technical knockout. (7) Anthony was too dazed to go on. He sure didn't see that coming. The world boxing heavy weight champion largely celebrated for his picture perfect fit body, agility and speed had been convincingly beaten by a "fat boy" whom no one gave a chance.

While everyone talked about the knockout suffered by Joshua, he was busy gathering knowledge on how best to confront his opponent in their rematch. He worked harder than ever and learnt that not all opponents would easily fall from his powerful punch. He didn't have to win every fight by knockout. He needed to get as much point as he possibly could while endeavouring to avoid being punched himself.

When the rematch finally came, we saw a totally different Joshua. Rather than close in on the opponent and throw hard punches in a bid to knock out Ruiz, he kept him at arm's length. He made use of his long arms, punching Ruiz from a distance while ensuring Ruiz didn't get close enough to punch him. He manifested a great deal of discipline staying the course through the 12 rounds, fighting in a pattern totally different from his usual way and eventually triumphing, having scored more points than Ruiz.(8)

He reclaimed his title as world champion because he gained knowledge when everyone focused on knockouts. If he concentrated on the knockout and let that take its toll on him, he would have bade final farewell to the top spot.

Winners learn from their mistakes. They know their failures can only be temporary because winning is their destiny. Time spent carefully studying the process to unravel the cause of failure rather than focus on the failure and letting it define you is crucial to your re-emergence as winner after a major slip. As long as you do not lose sight of the reality that you are a congenital winner and win you must, you wouldn't stay defeated for too long.

LARGESSE INSTEAD OF LOSSES

At some point in the relationship of Abraham and Lot, his nephew, they had some real strain that eventually led to them going their separate ways. The herdsmen of Abraham and those of Lot were having constant conflict because their livestock had become so many and they were frequently getting in each other's way.

Abraham as the older of the duo could have easily chosen the areas with the greenest pasture for his livestock, but he didn't. Rather, he gave Lot the opportunity to choose where he wanted while he settled in the other area. As expected, Lot chose the area that was most favourable for his livestock. An average person would have considered that as loss on Abraham's side. Abraham however, knew better than to think that way. Right after the separation, God told him to look as far as he could see in the four cardinal points of the earth and promised he would give him everything for his possession. He lost some hectares of lush grazing field in pursuit of peace and gained a limitless span of land in return from God.

Winners are not moved by the apparent losses occasioned by their right actions. They see the bountiful largesse underway rather than the immediate loss. Some of the richest men in the world today are into incredible charity activities. One would have thought since they are losing resources by giving so much, they would depreciate in wealth. The reverse is in fact true. The more they give, the richer they become. Every system on earth obeys the principle of sowing and reaping. The principle ensures that the harvest is multiple folds of the seed sown. You lose a seed in sowing, it appears the seed is forever lost. It however, comes back to you as a tree bearing numerous fruits with numerous seeds. Winners see the tree rather than the seed and that makes the loss of the seed inconsequential.

MOLEHILL RATHER THAN MOUNTAIN

Mount Everest is known to be the tallest mountain in the world. Its lofty 8,848m (20,029ft) elevation was thought to be insurmountable. Over the years, several explorers lost their lives while attempting to reach the summit of Everest. In fact, in 1924, George Mallory and Andrew Irvine made a summit attempt but they never returned. They were said to have disappeared in the clouds. Mallory's body was however discovered in 1999, about 75 years later on the north face of the mountain. As of 2019, over 300 people had died on Mt. Everest.

The life threatening hazards encountered en route the summit of the mountain naturally made it a mission impossible of some sort. This might have been the perception of most people, but certainly not the perception of Edmund Hillary and Tenzing Norgay who became the first people to officially ascend the Everest in 1953. (9) They disregarded the grim possibility of losing their lives on that mountain, ignored the wailing of the naysayers and chose to see a molehill instead of an impossible mountain. Of course, they succeeded.

As long as you keep magnifying the mountains confronting you and recounting how impossible surmounting them is, you will never surmount them. You must begin to minimize the mountain. You must begin to see yourself scaling that mountain and trampling it under your feet. You must begin to draw on the invincible nature of God within you which never cowers before any challenge but rather subdues and overcomes every challenge.

The winning nature of God deposited in us can surmount every mountain hindering our progress, but we need to learn to see through a winner's lens. We must see the mountains as molehills and nothing capable of contesting the measure of omnipotence resident in us.

NOVELTY RATHER THAN NOTHING

His name is John. He was referred to as "the beloved" because he was so fond of his Master and the feeling was mutual. Long after the death of his Master, he kept talking about the love of his Master and proclaiming his saving grace to whoever cared to listen. The ruling class that existed during the era he lived was however hostile to him and folks like him who were devoted to sharing the gospel of Jesus Christ

Due to his unrepentant commitment to spreading the message of Jesus despite several warnings to desist from doing so, he was banished to the Island of Patmos. For most people, that would have marked the end of their relevance. Banished to a lonely island, they would have lost their voice and spent the rest of their days in misery, believing nothing good can come out of that lonely island. In the case of John, the story was different. Rather than see nothing good in the Island, he in fact, saw a great vision of the glorified Christ and the events of the apocalypse. He received novel insights in eschatology.

Right in that lonely island, he wrote a new book titled Revelation, detailing the events of the last days and the ultimate destiny of the universe. The book was added to the cannon of scriptures and it is safe to call it an all-time bestseller as it continues to sell millions and millions of copies till date.

If John lacked the ability to see beyond the natural and look beyond his physical pain and allowed the unfortunate situation of his banishment and the hopeless situation of the island to get at him and dampen his spirit, he probably would have ended his days in defeat.

There is a possibility of novelty, a new beginning and a ground breaking idea in every island. Only those who exercise their senses to discern those not-so-apparent possibilities will emerge as winners even though we are all congenital winners.

OPEN DOORS RATHER THAN OBSTACLES

On that fateful day, he sat down by the road side, clad in his beggar's robe, asking alms of those who passed by. This had unfortunately become his routine since it dawned on him that there was no solution in sight to his blindness.

As he sat down helplessly hoping for alms, he perceived a great multitude was passing that way. When he inquired to know what was going on, he was informed that Jesus of Nazareth was passing by. Without waiting another second he began to cry out to Jesus saying, "Jesus thou son of David, have mercy on me." The man, who had come to be known as blind Bartimeus because he had been blind for almost his entire life and his blindness had come to be accepted as a way of identifying him, had heard that Jesus had the power to heal all manner of diseases. He therefore felt certain that if only he could get the attention of Jesus, his blindness will soon be history.

Unfortunately, as he kept calling for the attention of Jesus, some who felt he wasn't worth the attention of Jesus tried to hush him but rather than see the human obstacle trying to hinder him, he saw an open door into the restoration of his sight. He cried the more exceedingly until he was invited by Jesus and sure enough his sight was restored.

Any run-of-the-mill fellow could have resigned to fate and believe he was not meant to win back his sight due to the obstacles but such a person will never win even though he is a congenital winner and carries the winning gene in his genome.

Winners never accept no for an answer. They keep pushing until the goal is achieved. That unrelenting attitude is fertile ground for their winning genes to thrive.

POSSIBILITIES RATHER THAN PROBLEMS

Lionel Messi is a household name in the world of soccer. I dare say he requires no introduction. The Barcelona and Argentine superstar has made previously considered impossible feats in the world of football appear trivial as he achieves them almost effortlessly. He currently holds the record for the best male footballer of the year (6) and he doesn't appear to be slowing down at all.

Quite early in his life, Messi was diagnosed with Growth Hormone Deficiency and that was a great threat to his career as he was sickly and couldn't perform optimally. His then club, Newell's Old boys in Argentina had a chance to support his treatment and keep the future greatest player of all times, but they did not. Another club, River Plate, sought for him, but were equally driven away by the cost implications of his health challenge.

FC Barcelona however, saw the potential in this prodigy and looked beyond the problem. They signed him into their academy and helped pay for his treatment and now they've got the allegiance of the best player in the world. (10) The trophies he has helped them win have more than repaid whatever they spent on his treatment. Barcelona is one of the strongest clubs in the world today because they have Messi in their ranks. The same cannot be said of Newell's and River Plate.

Winners see possibilities rather than problems. Every problem is an avenue to exercise the winning potential that God has deposited in you. If you shrink away in fear, the potential remains dormant and unexpressed. If you however, take the problem head on and trust God for strength and wisdom to tackle it, you will surely win. Resolve never to run away from any challenge henceforth. Draw from the immense repository of power on the inside of you and winning will become your lifestyle. Philippians 4:13 says, "You can do all things through Christ who strengthens you." Halleluiah!

QUINTESSENCE RATHER THAN QUERIES

A winner sees quintessence where others see queries. This is beautifully illustrated in the biblical account of Apollos as recorded in Acts 18. Apollos was a born orator but had limited understanding of the word of God. He was only knowledgeable about the baptism of John but one couldn't help being mesmerized by his oratory gift.

Priscilla and Aquila on the other hand were sound and well-rounded believers who got to listen to Apollos and recognized the deficiencies in his theology.

They had the choice to focus on the queries that were apparent in the ministry of Apollos, but they chose rather to focus on the quintessential oratory prowess of the young man with a goal to balancing up what he lacked in knowledge so as to make him a well-rounded and highly productive minister. So they drew near to Apollos and taught him everything he needed to know about the ways of God. Did they achieve their goal? Of course, they did. Apollos became one of the greatest ministers in the early church. His oratory gift and his balanced understanding made him such an irresistible minister that he later came to be perceived as a rival to Apostle Paul himself as evidenced in 1 Corinthians 1:12.

Aquila and Priscilla saw the best in Apollos and made up their minds to stop at nothing until they perfected what was lacking in him and they succeeded. They all became winners in the end.

Choose to focus on the quintessence rather than the queries in your life and in others, while working towards bettering the areas of obvious deficiencies. You will always win.

RICHES RATHER THAN RAGS

Who would have thought that face masks will ever be an essential commodity to the general society? No one, frankly. However, the Covid-19 pandemic which created an overwhelming need for face masks and the inadequate supply of conventional masks to meet the ever increasing demand has made face masks hot cakes overnight.

The current legislation by heads of government making it illegal to step out of your house without putting on a face mask has equally accentuated the demand. In fact, you won't even be allowed access to health facilities or banking halls without a mask on in some places.

Some innovative thinkers have taken advantage of the situation to begin to sew fancy looking face masks from tiny pieces of clothes which would have been hitherto discarded as useless rags and they are making a fortune from the sale of those masks because of the high demand.

See, a winner doesn't see anything as useless. He recognizes what others consider rags a huge potential for riches and waits expectantly for an opportunity to explore the inherent potential in those seemingly useless rags. Of course, his investment always proves viable because nothing in God's universe is useless. Even the dung of animals can be profitably put to use as manure that supports the growth of crops. So when next you see rags, don't just trash them but recognize the riches that could proceed from them and you could be on your way to gaining a fortune.

SOLUTIONS RATHER THAN SUFFERING

Martin Luther King Junior was an American Christian minister and an activist who spearheaded the civil right movement. His primary goal was to abolish every form of segregation suffered by black Americans and ensure they enjoyed equal civil rights as their white counterparts. Everyone saw the pangs of segregation suffered by the Negroes and did nothing. Martin Luther King saw the sufferings but beyond them, a new dawn of hope and lasting solution to the problem.

His persuasion and uncommon vision drove him round the country leading nonviolent marches and protests in a bid to right the wrongs his people were subjected to. On one of such marches for freedom and jobs, on the steps of Lincoln Memorial in Washington, he gave his famous "I have a dream" speech (11) which emphasized his persuasion that a solution to their sufferings was underway. I have decided to put the full speech below to give you a glimpse of how a winner's mind works.

"I am happy to join with you today in what will go down in history as the greatest demonstration for freedom in the history of our nation.

Five score years ago a great American in whose symbolic shadow we stand today signed the Emancipation Proclamation. This momentous decree came as a great beckoning light of hope to millions of Negro slaves who had been seared in the flames of withering injustice. It came as a joyous daybreak to end the long night of their captivity.

But one hundred years later the Negro is still not free. One hundred years later the life of the Negro is still sadly crippled by the manacles of segregation and the chains of discrimination.

One hundred years later the Negro lives on a lonely island of poverty in the midst of a vast ocean of material prosperity.

One hundred years later the Negro is still languishing in the corners of American society and finds himself in exile in his own land.

We all have come to this hallowed spot to remind America of the fierce urgency of now. Now is the time to rise from the dark and desolate valley of segregation to the sunlit path of racial justice. Now is the time to change racial injustice to the solid rock of brotherhood. Now is the time to make justice ring out for all of God's children.

There will be neither rest nor tranquillity in America until the Negro is granted citizenship rights.

We must forever conduct our struggle on the high plane of dignity and discipline. We must not allow our creative protest to degenerate into physical violence. Again and again we must rise to the majestic heights of meeting physical force with soul force.

And the marvellous new militarism which has engulfed the Negro community must not lead us to a distrust of all white people, for many of our white brothers have evidenced by their presence here today that they have come to realize that their destiny is part of our destiny.

So even though we face the difficulties of today and tomorrow I still have a dream. It is a dream deeply rooted in the American dream.

I have a dream that one day this nation will rise up and live out the true meaning of its creed: 'We hold these truths to be self-evident; that all men are created equal."

I have a dream that one day on the red hills of Georgia the sons of former slaves and the sons of former slave owners will be able to sit together at the table of brotherhood.

I have a dream that one day even the state of Mississippi, a state sweltering with the heat of injustice, sweltering with the heat of oppression, will be transformed into an oasis of freedom and justice.

I have a dream that little children will one day live in a nation where they will not be judged by the colour of their skin but by the content of their character.

I have a dream today.

I have a dream that one day down in Alabama, with its vicious racists, with its Governor having his lips dripping with the words of interposition and nullification, one day right there in Alabama little black boys and black girls will be able to join hands with little white boys and white girls as sisters and brothers.

I have a dream today.

I have a dream that one day every valley shall be exalted, every hill and mountain shall be made low, the rough places plains, and the crooked places will be made straight, and before the Lord will be revealed, and all flesh shall see it together.

This is our hope. This is the faith that I go back to the mount with. With this faith we will be able to hew out of the mountain of despair a stone of hope. With this faith we will be able to transform the genuine discords of our nation into a beautiful symphony of brotherhood. With this faith we will be able to work together, pray together; to struggle together, to go to jail together, to stand up for freedom forever, knowing that we will be free one day.

And I say to you today my friends, let freedom ring. From the prodigious hilltops of New Hampshire, let freedom ring. From the mighty mountains of New York, let freedom ring. From the mighty Alleghenies of Pennsylvania!

Let freedom ring from the snow-capped Rockies of Colorado!

Let freedom ring from the curvaceous slopes of California!

But not only there; let freedom ring from the Stone Mountain of Georgia!

Let freedom ring from Lookout Mountain in Tennessee!

Let freedom ring from every hill and molehill in Mississippi. From every mountainside, let freedom ring.

And when this happens, when we allow freedom to ring, when we let it ring from every village and hamlet, from every state and every city, we will be able to speed up that day when all of God's children, black men and white men, Jews and Gentiles, Protestants and Catholics, will be able to join hands and sing in the words of the old Negro spiritual, "Free at last! Free at last! Thank God almighty, we're free at last!" (12)

What a speech! It was profound, persuasive, poignant, perspicacious and prophetic. In fact, in reaction to the speech, Jon Meacham wrote this, "With a single phrase, Martin Luther King Jr joined Jefferson and Lincoln in the ranks of men who have shaped modern America." (11)

His fight for civil rights and social justice for black Americans earned him Time Magazines Man of the year award for 1963 and 1964. He also became the youngest person to win a Nobel Peace Prize in 1964. Of course today the dream he had has come to fulfilment.

If he saw just the suffering but not the solution, he probably would have folded his arms in resignation to fate, leaving his people in perpetual suffering and dying in obscurity. His ability to see a ray of light at the end of the tunnel of segregation helped him navigate through the tunnel, thus forging a path to freedom for his race.

You too can become an agent of change. It all depends on what you choose to see. See the right things and you will not stop achieving great feats.

TRIUMPH RATHER THAN TRIBULATION

I know a man who lived many years ago, who suffered more tribulations than any of us could possibly imagine. He lost all his wealth in one day. He lost all his children, all his livestock and every single penny he had to his name. As though those were not enough, he was smitten with terrible boils from the crown of his head to the sole of his feet. Life was beyond horrible. He couldn't fathom what brought all those calamities upon him but rather than let himself be drowned in the depth of the raging storm, he chose to see triumph at the end of the tunnel.

He said in Job 19:25-26, *"For I know that my redeemer lives and that he shall stand in the latter day upon the earth: and though after my skin, worms destroy this body yet in my flesh shall I see God."*

Can you beat that? This man had hope beyond the grave! He was absolutely sure there was triumph coming for him at the end of his tribulation. He said in essence, even if I don't see that triumph in my life time, I will see it in death. Whether in death or in life, one thing is constant. I must triumph!

Did he triumph eventually? He sure did. Job 42:10 tells us, *"And the Lord turned away the captivity of Job when he prayed for his friends: also the Lord gave Job twice as much as he had before."*

See, Job came out of all his tribulations triumphant because he saw the possibility of triumph through the flame of his tribulations. He was absolutely sure his story was not going to end in the chapter of his tribulation. He could envision a glorious morning of triumph settling on the horizon and he lived to see that glorious day.

Do not allow your tribulations suck you in or get the better of you. Refuse to be preoccupied with the negative things going on in and around you. See triumph rather than tribulations and you will certainly emerge triumphant as long as you have the backing of the "God who always causes us to triumph in Christ and makes manifest the savour of his knowledge by us in every place."

UPGRADING RATHER THAN UNDOING

Daniel was well favoured by the King in Babylon because of his optimum productivity and impeccable character. His colleagues became jealous of him and wanted to pull him down by all means. They therefore set out on a search for some kind of fault in his life with which to incriminate him, but they found none.

When it became apparent to them that they wouldn't find any fault in Daniel except it had something to do with the worship of his God, they came up with a decree forbidding anyone from praying to any god apart from the king for 30 days. They knew Daniel would fall for that because nothing could come between him and the worship of his God. The King who was totally oblivious of their wicked scheme ignorantly signed the decree and thus gave the men a chance to see their expectation for Daniel materialize.

When Daniel discovered the decree had been signed, he wasn't bothered at all. He went to his house, opened his windows and prayed thrice daily to his God as was his usual practice. The men eventually apprehended him for contravening the king's decree and had him thrown into the den of lions. They obviously thought that was his final undoing.

Imagine their shock when the following day Daniel emerged from the lions' den unhurt and the king ordered that they all be thrown into the lions' den for their evil ploy to destroy Daniel. Of course, Christmas came early for the lions that day as they had more than enough flesh to devour. After that incident, the King recognized Daniel's God as supreme and his religion as superior. This resulted to Daniel being more favoured by the king which translated to an upgrade for him.

If Daniel had focused on the undoing which disobeying the King's decree could bring to him and succumbed to the pressure of worshipping the king rather than his God, he would have come to an unfortunate end. He however, saw the upgrade which comes to all who faithfully adhere to the worship of God and that led to his victory.

Perhaps the most compelling argument for the notion that people's names have a great impact on their lives is the case of the immediate past president of Nigeria, Dr Goodluck Ebele Jonathan. His steady rise from the position of Deputy Governor to Governor of Bayelsa state to Vice President of Nigeria and ultimately President of the Federal Republic seems nothing short of good luck.

However, in the run up to the 2015 general elections in which he sought a re-election for his 2nd term in office, he had so many factors contending against his re-election.

Amongst those was the growing dissatisfaction among the people with the level of insecurity in the country typified by the kidnapping of the Chibok girls by Boko Haram terrorists which brought about a global outcry. There was also widespread corruption among public office holders and an open discrediting of his government by Chief Olusegun Obasanjo due to a fall out between both of them.

When the elections finally came, Goodluck Jonathan eventually lost. As the incumbent president he had all the powers of the Commander in Chief at his disposal and could easily have rejected the result and held fast to the rein of power. He however recognized that there was a real danger of mass blood shed across the country should he refuse to concede defeat as the people in the opposition had threatened a carnage if their candidate lost. Previous events had proven that their threat was not an empty one as hundreds of people were killed in the previous elections which their candidate lost.

In his book "My Transition Hours", Dr Goodluck Jonathan described how much pressure he was under. He said, "I was in my living room with some of my ministers and advisors. They were recommending sundry alternatives but I was quiet in the midst of their discussion. I hugged my thoughts figuring out how to do that which was best for the country. My personal interest was receding rapidly and the interest of Nigeria loomed large. I excused myself and left the conference. I walked into my study. Even here my mantra was a strong circle around me, supporting and comforting me. What was that mantra? Let the country survive, let democracy survive, my political ambition is not worth the blood of any Nigerian."(13)

Armed with that conviction, he called the President - Elect, conceded defeat and handed over the rein of leadership to General Muhammadu Buhari. That singular act of patriotism and selflessness penned his name in gold in the annals of Nigeria's politics. He became the first African who conceded defeat as an incumbent president.

His defeat in the elections, though considered by some as his political undoing, has actually led to his upgrade. The legacy of peace which he left by his peaceful transfer of leadership earned him the position of Chairperson of the international summit council for Peace (ISCP) (14). He was also appointed by the United Nations as its special envoy on crises management. (15)

So, as it turns, what appeared as his undoing became the avenue for his upgrade from the national to the international stage because of his discernment that the path of peace and selflessness is the path to progress.

VICTORY RATHER THAN VULNERABILITY

Nicholas James Vujicic must have felt terrible when he was old enough to recognize for the first time that he actually had no limbs like other normal children. He was born with a rare condition known as Tetra Amelia Syndrome (Phocomelia), which meant he had no hands and legs. His mother struggled to accept him when she gave birth to him and later, both his parent later accepted him, believing God had a plan for his life. He himself even considered suicide once.

Rather than focus on his disabilities and the vulnerabilities warranted by them, he decided to accept his condition as part of God's plan and made up his mind to achieve all he could in spite of his disability. By the help of God and his discernment of his victory despite his vulnerabilities, he went to college and graduated with a Bachelor of Commerce with a double major in Accountancy and Finance Planning. He is a Christian evangelist and motivational speaker. He is an author. He was awarded best actor in a short film for his role in the film, "The Butterfly Circus". He is the founder of "Life without Limbs" an international non-profit organization and "Attitude is Altitude", a secular motivational speaking company. (16) He is also married to a beautiful wife and is a happy father. What else is there to achieve?

If Nick could achieve all these without hands and legs, you certainly can achieve whatever God has made you for. Look away from your vulnerability; focus on the victory that lies ahead of you and you will surely win because you are a congenital winner.

WINNERS RATHER THAN WANDERERS

At a point in the life of David, an assembly of about 400 men came to him. They were people in distress, people in debt and people discontented. If you call them frustrated wanderers you won't be totally wrong. This crop of men came to David to be their leader. Any other person could have considered the present profile of the men and turned down their demand because of their apparently little prospects, but David was different. He saw in them a band of mighty winners despite their unattractive situation. He gathered them together and became their captain.

These men eventually rose to become such mighty men of valour that were able to surpass the military might of David himself. One of them held to his sword and slew so many to the point that the sword clave to his hand. With a single spear another one killed 200 men. On a certain day, David asked to drink water from the waters of Bethlehem before which was a host of Philistine armies. Three of David's men ran through the host of the Philistines, got the water and brought it to David. They were almost invincible warriors. David enjoyed the benefits of their valour because he saw the winner in them when they didn't look like it. He discerned the winner in them when they appeared like hopeless wanderers.

What do you see when you look at people? Do you see potential helpers or perpetual wanderers? What you see can significantly affect what you eventually get. See the right thing by the help of God's Spirit and you won't miss your helpers in Jesus name.

X-FACTOR RATHER THAN XENOPHOBIA

Sometime in 2019, the term Xenophobia was all over the internet because of the ill treatment of Nigerian residents in South Africa. Nigerians were attacked, some murdered, and their properties burnt because some delinquent South Africans just couldn't tolerate the presence of the foreigners in their country. Everyone saw the evil of the xenophobic attacks and decried it but didn't see a solution out of it.

However, a man by the name of Allen Onyema, the Chief Executive Officer of Peace Airline, didn't just focus on the xenophobic attacks but saw a way out of the quagmire for his compatriots.

He dispatched his airlines to South Africa and evacuated 503 Nigerians. He brought them back home to their native country thus liberating them from the torture of their oppressors (17) and instantly became a national hero for that patriotic act.

The X-Factor is the solution to a problem. In Mathematics you are given an equation and told to solve for X. That X in Mathematics translates to the solution to difficult problems which seem elusive. Allen Onyema saw the difficult equation posed by Xenophobia and focused on seeking the X-Factor which is the solution to the problem, while others sat back and lamented the difficult nature of the equation. Of course, when he won fame and accolades for his heroic acts, all the other people sat back as spectators.

Your ability to discern the solution to difficult situations will set you apart from your peers. Don't just focus on the problem. Don't just lament and criticize. Sit back, critically analyse the situation and trust God for inspiration, and you will surely find the solution. When you are a solution provider, you are bound to be relevant wherever you go.

YIELD RATHER THAN YOKES

Before the advent of vehicles and carriage vans, farmers had to carry their produce on their heads from the farm to the market where those produce are sold. Of course, the bigger the load they carry, the more arduous the journey to the market.

Some losers might consider the difficulty of the journey and decide to quit but never a winner. A winner focuses on the yield that awaits him when he sells those produce at the market rather than the yoke constituted by the load on him. His hope for maximum yield keeps him going until he arrives the market, sells his goods and makes his profit.

Your potential for winning though definite, can be undermined by your undue consideration of yokes and desire for ease. If you however recognize that "it is good for a man that he bear the yoke in his youth" (Lamentations 3:27), and you keep trudging on to your goal, you will have maximum yield.

The same concept applies to investment. When people invest their resources into a certain venture, they invariably have to suffer some temporary inconveniences. The lack of convenience could be considered a yoke but you must understand that your yield is buried in that yoke. If you bear the yoke and make the investment and things work well, you eventually receive the yield. If you however decide to live for the moment saying, "let's eat and drink for tomorrow we die", hunger will most definitely be the cause of your death tomorrow.

Think of it spiritually, Jesus Christ has offered his life to save us from our sins and he calls us to bear his yoke which by the way is light. His yoke entails staying away from evil and it promises a yield of eternal life with God in heaven. You know there are people who would rather refuse to bear the yoke of Christ because they prefer to enjoy the pleasure of sin, at the risk of losing their soul in hell. If you however choose to deny yourself the pleasures of sin and bear the yoke of Christ till the end then you are guaranteed his eternal yield of unending joy in God's kingdom.

ZENITH RATHER THAN ZERO

There was a charming young lady by the name Esther whose beauty was breathtaking. She lost her parents at a very tender age and so had to be brought up by her uncle. Esther and her uncle were living in an empire to which the Jews had been taken as captives, so they more or less amounted to zeroes as far as social status was concerned.

Her beauty regardless, Esther humbled herself and imbibed the values of chastity, candour and charity taught her by her uncle and she was confident she was headed for the zenith in spite of her present circumstance. Her focus on reaching the zenith prevented her from meddling with low lives who would have derailed her.

As God would have it, the opportunity for her lifting came when the King of the entire empire began to seek a wife. The moment he set his eyes on Esther he could tell she was a lady prepared for the throne. Without much ado, she was crowned the Queen of the entire empire. So, in the twinkling of an eye, she rose from being a Zero with whom no one reckoned to being the First Lady in the kingdom to whom everyone deferred. Can you beat that? It all happened because she looked beyond her peasant status and saw the bigger picture which contained God's purpose for her life, and she walked right into it.

What do you think about yourself? Do you see yourself as a Zero or as one made for the zenith? It matters a lot because "as a man thinks in his heart so is he"(Proverbs 23:7).

Quit thinking small! Quit the petty living! See the bigger picture! You were created for much more!

Start living out God's dream for your life. You are a congenital winner. Start thinking and living as one. I will be the first to celebrate you when the news of your breakthrough comes out. See you at the top!

CHAPTER 4
THE DISCIPLINE OF A WINNER

"Discipline is the bridge between goals and accomplishment."

-Jim Rohn

As a young undergraduate student in the University of Babylon, Daniel and his friends were faced with the pressure of indulging their appetites for the dainties served at the King's palace. The meals were sacrificed to the gods of the land and as such eating such food was against the values and faith by which they were raised. They had the choice of ignoring their upbringing and enjoying themselves at the risk of provoking the ire of their God or denying themselves the pleasure of partaking in those meals at the risk of the King's displeasure.

Daniel knew where he was coming from and knew his goal was to reach the top. He was also aware that to reach his goal, he couldn't afford to eat and indulge himself like anyone else. So together with his friends, he decided he would not eat of the king's dainties.

A Winner's Discipline Of His Appetite

Daniel 1:8 says, "Daniel purposed in his heart, that he will not defile himself with the portion of the King's meat or with the wine which he drank, so he requested of the Prince of the Eunuchs, that he might not defile himself."

Even though the King's meat and wine served to the students was enticing and alluring, Daniel and his friends preferred to eat pulse and drink water so they could focus on achieving their goals rather than enjoy the luxury of the King's meat and alter their sensibilities by the wine which he drank. Daniel and his friends had a grip on their appetites and that made them go far.

At the end of their study period, when they were examined, they aced all their courses. In fact, they were ten times better than their counterparts who were busy having the time of their life munching meat and gulping wine.

If you will live out your potential as a winner, you must have discipline over your appetite. You can't afford to just eat whatever you are offered or drink whatever you are offered. Scriptures say, "He that strives for mastery is temperate in all things" (1 Corinthians 9:25). In other words to be a master in your chosen career, you must exercise self-control. You must have a grip on your appetite in other to excel in all your endeavours.

Many people eat compulsively and get obese. Obesity by itself is capable of reducing productivity because it makes people too heavy to move themselves about. It also predisposes people to health disorders like diabetes, hypertension, heart disease and stroke.

All of these things will ultimately prevent you from becoming the winner that you were born to be. You can however prevent them from getting to you by disciplining your appetite.

Eat just enough to keep you going and nothing more. Say no to gluttony. Even when there is so much to eat, eat smart because you are not a commoner, you are a winner.

A WINNER'S DISCIPLINE OF HIS PASSIONS

There was a powerful man by the name of Samson who had the strength of a dozen men or maybe more. He was anointed by God to be the deliverer of his people Israel from the oppression of the Philistines. His power was out of this world. He killed a lion with his bare hands, killed a thousand men with the jawbone of an ass and pulled out the gate of a city together with its pillars singlehandedly. He however had an untamed passion for women.

Like a beast without control, Samson allowed his passion run wild searching for different kinds of women and sowing his wild oats until he eventually landed in the arms of Delilah who pressed him to the point of disclosing the source of his power.

Once she discovered his power resided in his unshaved hair, she made him sleep, shaved his hair and by the time Samson woke up he was as light as dust. All his powers had gone. What a tragedy! His eyes were plucked out and he was made a laughing stock to the Philistines.

On the other hand, we have a man named Joseph who faced a serious temptation to sleep with his master's wife. His master was a high ranking officer in Pharaoh's army. Of course, a man of that standing will definitely have a good looking wife. So it wasn't as though an ugly woman was pestering Joseph to lie with her. It was a really beautiful woman with influence and power who was capable of impacting the fortunes of Joseph that was wooing him to the bed.

Considering the fact that such a woman was making advances on him on a daily basis, Joseph must have felt some urges in his body which his flesh would have been willing to satisfy. He must have had a nagging feeling to just do it and forget about the consequences but he reminded himself that it would amount to wickedness in the sight of God to sleep with his master's wife and he knew that would effectively abort his dream of becoming great. So he shunned the idea and focused on his work.

On a certain day when no one else was in the house, the woman grabbed Joseph as though saying, "Today is the day. You must lie with me before leaving this place." When Joseph recognized he couldn't trust his body to do right if he stayed too long in the grip of that seductress, he had to forcefully pull away from her leaving his cloth with her, and dashed out of the house as quickly as his legs could carry him. That is the discipline of someone who is bent on winning at all cost.

If you want to get to the top, you cannot afford to be controlled by your genitals. You cannot afford to gratify every base desire you feel. You have to keep your hormones in check so they don't end up driving you out of relevance.

Samson is arguably the strongest man to have lived, but his life became a disaster because of his untamed passion. Joseph, on the other hand was not so strong but he rose to become a Prime Minister because he had discipline over his passions.

In whose camp are you? The Samson camp or the Joseph camp? It will determine exactly where your life will end. Do not waste the potential God has deposited in you because you want to satisfy some transient feelings. The pleasure you derive from that romp is not worth your destiny which you are giving in exchange for it. Be wise! Flee fornication! Master your passions, don't let them master you. God's grace is available to help you overcome every sexual addiction. Call upon Jesus! He will set you free and enable you live the winning life he created you to live.

A Winner's Discipline Of His Eyes

In the seventh chapter of the book of Joshua, there is the account of a shock defeat suffered by the Israelites at the hands of a relatively small foe which they actually underestimated. Some of them had been sent to spy the land of Ai and what they saw made them confident there was no need taking the entire army to fight such a small enemy. Their recommendation was that 2000 or 3000 soldiers were more than enough to defeat Ai.

To their utter disbelief, their army was overpowered by the enemy soldiers and they took to their heels eventually losing about thirty-six of their soldiers. When inquiries were made about the cause of their defeat, they discovered that a man by the name of Achan was responsible.

When he was compelled to confess his misdeed, he said he saw a goodly Babylonian garment, 200 shekels of silver and a wedge of gold worth 50 shekels. Seeing those things wasn't the problem. He kept looking at them until he began to covet them; that is, he was having an inordinate desire to possess them. That led him to steal those things and hide them in his tent. That singular act made the entire army lose the favour of God which had been responsible for their previous victories, thus exposing them to a disgraceful defeat.

There are many people today who have no control over their eyes. They spend countless hours watching movies, surfing the internet, watching pornography and other unwholesome sights. Such people cannot amount to much in life.

A determined winner disciplines his eyes. You cannot set your eyes on anything that doesn't contribute towards making you the winner that you've been destined to be. You cannot allow your eyes enslave you to the point you just follow it wherever it goes as a lamb to the slaughter. You must be the boss of your life. Take charge of what you see and for how long you see them. Even legitimate things should not be viewed for too long. You are a man on a mission, you must be conscious of time. Never fall for the temptation to covet what belongs to someone else. That is the attitude of losers. Winners are contented with what they have and are confident that their resources will suffice to take them to the top where they will find every other treasure they seek.

It was Job who said "I made a covenant with my eyes why then should I think upon a maid" (Job 31:1). In other words, he was saying I have made up my mind to discipline my eyes and never allow it to lead me to look lustfully at a woman, or anything else for that matter. No wonder he was such a great man. Discipline yourself like he did and you will also express the fruits of the seed of greatness that was planted in you at your creation.

A WINNER'S DISCIPLINE OVER SLEEP

Inarguably, the greatest winner to ever walk the earth is the Lord Jesus Christ. He gives us the perfect model of control over sleep.

Mark 1:45 gives us a glimpse at his daily routine. It says, "And in the morning, rising up a great while before day, he went out and departed into a solitary place and there prayed." Talk of commitment to your purpose!

Jesus knew he had an uncommon assignment; he couldn't afford to sleep like common men. He woke up a great while before day to start praying and planning for the day's work. All winners are early risers. You can't be hoping to be a winner and be sleeping like a log of wood. If daybreak meets you on your bed, you are not doing well.

You should sleep early so you can rise early and utilise the quietness of the early hours of the day to pray, meditate, commune with God and strategize on how to go about achieving your goal for that day. Your ability to achieve daily set milestones is what will eventually take you to the top where you desire to be.

There is no prize for best sleeper. If you keep changing the gear of your sleep while others are up building value into their lives, you will end up being a spectator when they are celebrated.

Proverbs 6:9-11 says, "How long wilt thou sleep, o sluggard? When wilt thou arise out of thy sleep? Yet a little sleep, a little slumber, a little folding of the hands to sleep: So shall thy poverty come as one that travelleth and thy want as an armed man."

You know what this means? It's saying just like a travelling man must reach his destination so must poverty arrive at the house of the perpetual sleeper. You know how an armed man holds you hostage and there is no way of escape, so is there no way a perpetual sleeper can escape want. Cut down on your sleep and do something meaningful with your life. You will surely win in Jesus name!

CHAPTER 5
THE DILIGENCE OF A WINNER

"Seeth thou a man diligent in his business? He shall stand before Kings, he shall not stand before mean men."

-Proverbs 22:29

A GLIMPSE AT BOLT

Usain Bolt is a Jamaican former sprinter who is largely considered as the fastest man that ever lived. He holds the world records for 100m, 200m and 4×100m relay.

He is an eight-time Olympic gold medallist and the only sprinter to have won Olympic 100m and 200m titles at 3 consecutive Olympics. He is an eleven time world champion and he is the most successful athlete in the world. How did he achieve all these great feats? Did they just happen to him? Did he stumble on so much success and fame? Not likely.

The success of Usain Bolt was the product of diligence. Among other factors, hard work played a crucial role in getting him to the top of his career.

He is said to hit the gym every morning for a 90-minute workout session which is geared towards improving his speed and agility while maintaining an athletic body. He didn't find them funny. In fact, if he had his way he would have stayed away from the gym but he kept at it in order to fulfil his dream.

Apart from his really tasking gym sessions, he had to go through several sprint drills under the supervision of his coach to keep him on top of his game. His coach was a perfectionist to the core and nothing Bolt did seemed good enough. He kept pushing him to outdo himself over and over again. He was quoted as saying "Every race I ran, I thought it was the perfect race, then coach Mills told me 'no'. When I ran a world record the first time, I was like: yeah coach you see that, that is a good record but that was no good. Even in the Olympics, I was like start was good, no? He was like 'no'. Every time I think I do something great, he tells me I have more to do." (18)

You see he was constantly being pushed to the limits. He kept working his butt off and in the end it paid off. You cannot be the winner you were born to be by folding your arms and doing nothing. Proverbs 21:25 says, "The desire of the slothful killeth him for his hand refuses to labour."

To be the winner you were born to be, you must imbibe the culture of hard work. Put your nose to the grindstone and labour long and hard to achieve your set goals. That is one of the cornerstone ethics of every winner that has walked the earth. If you want to join the line of winners you must follow suit.

Gleaning From Jesus

If there was one person who epitomized diligence in his life work, it was Jesus. Hard work was almost second nature to him. He literally lived to work. Diligence was an imperative in his life.

One time, his parents had taken him for their annual feast at Jerusalem. At the end of the feast, they packed their luggage and left for home supposing that Jesus was with them. By the time they discovered he was not in their company, they became worried and almost in a frenzy looking everywhere for him. They later found him in the temple at Jerusalem interacting with the doctors. When his mother announced to him that they had been looking everywhere for him, his response was: "How is it that ye sought me, know ye not that I must be about my Fathers business?"

Wow! Just in case you forgot, it will help to recall that he was only 12 years old at the time. How many twelve-year- olds have you met who are that business oriented? His work ethic was simply unparalleled.

There were times he spent the entire night praying then went about normal routine, teaching, preaching and healing folks in the course of the day. When the disciples thought he should be tired and in need of some rest, he would tell them, "I must preach the kingdom of God to other cities also: for therefore am I sent." You see, he was all about doing the work he was sent to do. He had no time to sit idle, lazy about and just engage in endless banters. He was on a mission and every calorie of energy in him was expended fulfilling that mission.

At another instance, he was quoted as saying, "I must work the works of him that sent me while it is day: the night cometh when no man can work." Can you beat that? He was saying, "Hey! Why will I be idle when it's still day time? Day is for work and I must be seen working as long as it is day. When night falls I won't be able to do much. So I have to arise and make hay while the sun shines, else I will suffer loss." Are you learning anything from him?

If you work hard and long the way he did, you will definitely win the way he won. If you decide to eat the bread of idleness or play all day, you will definitely walk the sorrow strewn path of losers even though you are a congenital winner.

GIVING YOUR ALL

Winning the ultimate prize will demand nothing less than your all. You cannot be haphazard and wishy-washy in your approach to your job and expect to be a winner. You will end up being a frustrated loser. To maximize your potential as a congenital winner, you must put your all into everything you do. Be a 100 percent individual who ensures 100 percent of your abilities and intellectual powers are fully engaged in the execution of any task you are given. The outcome will always be marvellous.

Ecclesiastes 9:10 says "Whatsoever thy hand findeth to do, do it with thy might; for there is no work nor device, nor knowledge nor wisdom in the grave wither thou goest." So you need not spare any ounce of energy in the execution of any task you undertake. Employ all your might in performing your job. Your might is relevant as long as you are alive. Once you die, it is useless. How well you use it now, will determine how you will be remembered.

If you are praying, pray like your life depends on it. If you are studying, study like your life depends on it. If you are executing any task do it like your life depends on it. Engage every faculty you've got in executing every task you undertake, there is no way you won't excel. No skill or gift should be left unutilized in the pursuit of your dream. Keep working! Never quit! You will surely win!

CHAPTER 6
THE DOGGEDNESS OF A WINNER

---

*"Great works are performed not
by strength but by perseverance."*

- Samuel Johnson

THE PICTURE OF DOGGEDNESS

In Judges Chapter 8, the story of Gideon and his 300-man army chasing after the army of Midian was told. The Midianite army led by their two kings - Zebah and Zalmuna had been a thorn in the flesh of the Israelites and now Gideon was going to make them pay dearly.

In the course of the battle, Gideon and his men had a hard time pursuing after the Midianites. Judges 8:4 gives a vivid picture of their ordeal. It says, "And Gideon came to Jordan and passed over, he and the three hundred men that were with him, faint, yet pursuing them"

They were feeling faint, famished and were being fagged by the process but they knew if they had to win, they must keep pursuing. They had come too far to back out. There was just no way they would go back without getting the decisive victory which they needed. That is doggedness.

The journey to greatness is never a smooth cruise. There are numerous crests and troughs, ups and downs, bumps, bends and countless detours to ensure you don't make it to your destination. To be the winner you were born to be, you must keep running your race in spite of the odds until you reach the finish mark.

Gideon and his men had every reason to quit pursuing their enemies. For God's sake they were fainting, their lives were at stake. Anyone would have understood if they called it a day and returned home. Maybe that's true but they would have been denied the fulfilment that comes with winning and they would have lived to fight another day because their enemies would reinforce and come back for them.

No reason for quitting the pursuit of your God-given dream is good enough. You must exercise every nerve in your body to the limit in the pursuit of your dream. Keep at it until you complete it.

THE PAIN OF DOGGEDNESS

When you choose to remain dogged in the pursuit of your dreams against all odds, you are bound to experience some pain. In the case of Gideon and his men, they suffered the pain of resentment and rejection.

In the course of their pursuit, when their hunger became unbearable, Gideon and his men made recourse to the men of Succoth to assist them with something to eat. The Princes of Succoth blatantly refused to help them. They asked them, "Are the hands of Zebah and Zalmuna now in thine hands that we should give bread to thine army?" In other words, they were saying, "What have you achieved to make us want to give you our bread?" Why should we give you our bread, when you are not even guaranteed a win in your present battle?

Gideon and his men left those men and went to the men of Penuel to seek help and yet again, they were mercilessly denied any form of help. They had to continue their pursuit of victory, hungry and exhausted.

More often than not when you are resolved to win at all costs, you get to suffer pain in the process. It could come in the form of resentment from people who do not believe in your ability to achieve anything meaningful or rejection from people to whom you look for assistance, who however do not consider you worthy of their assistance.

People will laugh at you, make fun of you and some may even prophesy doom for you. If you do not let their pessimism deter you, you will eventually reach your goal. By all means try to prevent the negativity of the naysayers from getting to you. If you quit your pursuit, you would have proven them right. So if for nothing else, to prove them wrong, keep running until you reach your destination.

While writing the book in your hand, I had to endure some pain. There were times my buttocks ached from sitting for long and then I periodically would have to get on my knees. After some time, my knees would begin to hurt and I won't be comfortable on my knees anymore and then I would lie on the bed and later go back to sit. It wasn't easy at all, but because I had targets to meet, I kept writing. I was dogged in my determination to finish the book and fulfil my dream of being an author and, beyond that, of impacting the lives of other people so they can go ahead and be the winners God created them to be.

THE PRIZE OF DOGGEDNESS

Gideon and his men refused to be discouraged or deterred from their pursuit, in spite of the pain they suffered along the way. In the end, they caught up with the Midianite host, discomfited the entire army and took their two kings as prisoners of war. Of course, they eventually killed them.

When Gideon returned from the battle, he was immediately catapulted to the status of a national hero. In fact, the people unanimously decided to make him their king, but he turned down the offer. He, however, remains a legend for his military prowess. If Gideon and his men had quit due to the difficulties they encountered in the course of their pursuit, they would not have won. Gideon would be forgotten. His name would have disappeared into oblivion. No one would reckon with him or his family. He would have left no mark on the sand of time. We remember him today because he was dogged. He persevered and kept running the race until he won.

You too can become a hero. There is nothing Gideon had that you do not have. You have one head with two eyes, a nose and a mouth just like he had. You have two arms and two legs just like he had. He has the winning potential breathed into him by God which you also have. Conversely, there are many things you have that he didn't have. You have the benefit of a much more sophisticated educational system, you have access to advanced technologies and you have access to the internet which is an almost unlimited store of information, all of which Gideon didn't have. If he was able to succeed, you have no excuse not to succeed.

You need to develop doggedness in the pursuit of your goals. Let nothing deter you from reaching your targets. Trust God for grace to run your race until the end. That's what congenital winners do.

You must grow your staying power. That is the ability to keep at a task until it is completed. There are many individuals who start really laudable projects but lack the doggedness to see it through to completion. The man who gets celebrated is not the one who starts a project but never gets to finish it. The man who gets celebrated is the one who begins a project and keeps at it against all odds until it is completed because like the holy bible says, "Better is the end of a thing than the beginning thereof" (Ecclesiastes 7:8).

CHAPTER 7
THE DISCIPLESHIP OF A WINNER

"Mentoring is a brain to pick,
an ear to listen and a push in
the right direction."

-John Crosby

THE NEED FOR DISCIPLESHIP

Young Samuel had been returned to Eli the Priest to spend the rest of his life in the service of God as his mother had vowed. Still as green as a gooseberry, Samuel had many things to learn in his new career, the greatest of which was hearing the voice of God.

One night while he lay down to sleep, God called his name. Being a novice in the business, he ran to Eli his master, thinking he was the one who called him. Eli told him he didn't call him, and that he could return to his bed. This happened again and again until Eli perceived it was God calling Samuel at which point he instructed him on what to say in order to hear what God had to say.

Left to Samuel, he probably would have kept running to and fro without being able to discern God's voice even if

God called a dozen times. Therein lies the need for mentorship or discipleship.

As a prospective winner, you have great potential no doubt, but you need someone who is an established winner, who has garnered all manner of experiences from winning several battles to help you maximize your potential and make a winner out of you.

All around us today, we see the tragedy of an "unmentored" generation. Young men and women who would have been great achievers end up being thugs, prostitutes and never-do-wells because they lacked the privilege of proper discipleship. Able bodied men who could have turned out to be erudite scholars if properly discipled end up becoming armed robbers and kidnappers due to lack of discipleship.

A child left to himself is a disaster waiting to happen. Except someone goes out of his way to stoop to the level of young people and endeavour to lead them in the right way through his words and deeds, society will have a really negative impact on their lives and they will end up becoming delinquents rather than the winners they were born to be.

Ralph Waldo Emerson said, "Our chief want in life is somebody who will make us do what we can." That somebody is what many people lack and that's why they fail to live out the winning potential resident in them. The challenge is not that they can't do it but they lack someone to motivate them and make them realize that all they need to become who they want to be has been put in them by God right from the day they were conceived in their mother's womb.

How about you, my dear friend? Do you have a mentor? Are you someone's disciple? Do you have that coach in your life who is constantly pushing you to be a better you and scale the utmost heights? If not, why not? We all need mentors to help us be who we were made to be. Endeavour to get a mentor and you will be glad you did, that is if you get the right one.

THE NATURE OF AN IDEAL MENTOR

It was Benjamin Franklin who said, "Tell me and I forget, teach me and I may remember, involve me and I learn."

Paul the Apostle, perhaps one of the greatest mentors to have lived was writing to Timothy his mentee, and he said, "But thou hast fully known my doctrine, manner of life, purpose, faith, longsuffering, charity, patience."

Do you see that? An ideal mentor hides nothing from his mentee. The ideal mentor reveals every winning strategy he has up his sleeves to his disciple because he desires above all things to see his disciple succeed.

The ideal mentor is a God-fearing person of undisputable character. This is very important because there have been cases where people have been sexually abused and molested by supposed mentors. You do not want that to happen to you so you must be very careful when selecting a mentor. It is suggested that your mentor be someone of the same gender as you. Even then, still ensure they are people of sound character.

An ideal mentor should be available and approachable. There is no use having a mentor whom you can't reach. A mentor is someone you can reach out to just about any time and he will be ready to talk to you and proffer solutions to your challenges. You can also have distant mentors. That is people who are beyond your reach but whom you can learn from by reading their books and perhaps listening to their audio resources.

An ideal mentor should be a winner himself. You have no business meeting a serial failure for discipleship. What exactly do you want to learn from him, how to fail? Of course, not. So, you should carefully seek someone who has a reputation for consistent winning and tag along with him or her to glean from his or her wealth of knowledge.

An ideal mentor should be selfless and sacrificial. He should be ready to deny himself some privileges for the benefit of his disciples. He should be ready to spend his resources to assist his disciples in reaching their goals. He doesn't consider any price too high to pay for the success of his disciples.

The best mentor there is anywhere in the world is the Lord Jesus Christ himself. He is the embodiment of the above characteristics and much more. He died on the cross of Calvary to save us from our sins. He redeemed us from the curse of the law which perpetually limited us and made every hope of winning a mirage. He was made poor that we through his poverty might become rich. You can't find a better mentor than Him. Sign up for His discipleship by asking Him into your life right now and you would have made the greatest decision of your life. He will guide you to other worthy human mentors who will help make your journey to the top easier

THE MERITS OF DISCIPLESHIP

The merits of discipleship are many. If you pick your mentor wisely, you are bound to enjoy these gains. Firstly, you will avoid the pitfalls that your mentors experienced on their way to the top. A sincere mentor will not hide challenges encountered from his mentees. By revealing those challenges to his mentees and educating them on how he was able to overcome them, the mentees would easily scale over those challenges.

A mentee has the privilege of standing on the shoulder of his mentor and is thus given the advantage of a higher field of vision. As such, he is positioned to go well beyond the achievements of his mentor.

Furthermore, since the mentee has the constant motivation and push from his mentor, he is not likely to quit pursuing his goals as would someone without a mentor. Even if he gets discouraged and feels no motivation to keep working on his goal, he will get the needed push from his mentor and return to his feet again.

There is also the added advantage of financial support from a financially buoyant mentor to fund the projects of the mentee, should the need arise.

Finally there is the joy of having a trusted friend to rejoice with when your dream eventually comes through. The feeling is priceless. Knowing that this person has stuck with you through the ups and downs of your journey and kept cheering you on till the last minute when you eventually won the crown brings an incredible feeling of gratitude and affection.

Therefore, by all means be a disciple of a worthy mentor and you will most definitely maximize your potential as a congenital winner.

CHAPTER 8
THE DEFERENCE OF A WINNER

"A man who pays respect to the great, paves the way for his own greatness."

-African Proverb

PRECISE UNDERSTANDING OF DEFERENCE

You know I find the life of Joseph inspiring in many ways. I believe he is a good example of deference. I mean, Joseph was humble and respectful to the core.

Even though Joseph had a dream of the sun, the moon and eleven stars bowing to him, which meant he was destined to be superior to all his family members in greatness, he was still humble and respectful enough to run errands for his father and subject himself to the leadership of his older siblings. There wasn't a single disrespectful or rebellious bone in that young man.

When his brothers wickedly sold him into slavery, he could have been bitter and full of hate thus losing his coolheaded nature and his deference for people but rather than do that, he remained as cool as a cucumber. It showed in the way he behaved himself in the house of Potiphar.

He was so respectful and loyal to his master that his master had to commit everything in his house to Joseph's care. He ran all the businesses of Potiphar, decided what went out and what came in and determined who got what. Not a bad position for someone who was sold as slave to a foreign land you know! Deference will take you places you never imagined possible.

When Joseph was falsely accused by Potiphar's wife, an allegation that eventually landed him in prison; he proved once again that his deference was not limited to men of high societal standing, but to everyone. He was just as respectful of his fellow inmates and the prison wardens as he was respectful of Potiphar, his master. He was respectful enough to listen to the dreams of the prison wardens and provide interpretations to their dreams even though he himself was a victim of the inhumanity of men and had his own dreams on the line.

It was Albert Einstein who said, "I speak to everyone in the same way, whether he is the garbage man or the President of the university." Do you wonder why he was that great? Deference will take you where intelligence can't take you. What if you come up with an invention and the appropriate licensing bodies refuse to accept it because of your arrogance? Every effort you make meets a brick wall because people cannot just put up with your brand of egocentrism. You will eventually die a frustrated fellow in spite of your intelligence.

Respect for those ahead of you and indeed everyone must be part of your paraphernalia as you embark on the pursuit of greatness. You need people to get to where you are going and you cannot get them on your side unless you truly respect them. The Holy Bible says, "Pride goes before destruction and an haughty spirit before a fall" (Proverbs 16:18).

God himself "resists the proud but gives grace to the humble" (James 4:6). Imagine God is resisting a man, what can such a man ever amount to in life?

PRACTICE OF DEFERENCE IN PURSUIT OF GREATNESS

Just like any skill can be honed by consistent practice, you can better your expression of deference by practice. Joseph had practiced deference from his father's place to the pit, to Pharaoh's house and in the prison. By the time he got before Pharaoh in the palace, he didn't have to take a crash course on deference in order to properly address the King. He had perfected the act of deference so his conversation with Pharaoh was fluid. Pharaoh couldn't help being impressed by his courtesy despite his profound insight.

You know there are individuals who because of some small gifts think they are better than everyone else. They can no more listen to their parents or senior colleagues because they feel they know better. Such people cannot go far. Providence always endeavours to bring them down because bad followers cannot make good leaders.

For you who are intent on expressing your winning potential, you must be respectful of those who have gone ahead of you and those around you. It begins with your attitude. The way you relate with people is a product of what you think about yourself and them.

God's words says, "Let no man think of himself more highly than he ought to think, but to think soberly" (Romans 12:3).

Philippians 2:3 says, "Let nothing be done through strife or vainglory but in lowliness of mind let each esteem others better than themselves."

That is the kind of attitude that helps you defer to others. When you do not have an over bloated perception of who you are and consider others better than yourself, you will naturally defer to people. The more you practice deference to others whether young or old, illiterate or literate, rich or poor, the more you will be respected and the closer you will get to greatness.

David was anointed to be King of Israel as a teenager but even though he was fully aware of his imminent coronation, he was still humble enough to run errands for his father and tend his father's flock of sheep. He didn't say, "Don't you know I'm the future king? How can you be sending me to do such a humiliating job?" Instead, he humbled himself and deferred to his father.

At some point in his life, Saul was desperately after his life. As fate would have it, one of the days Saul lay helplessly asleep together with all his soldiers around him after intense fatigue from pursuing an innocent boy. That would have been the perfect opportunity for David to kill Saul and take over the throne but he still deferred to him as the anointed of the Lord. He ended up just cutting a part of Saul's skirt as a proof to Saul that he could have killed him if he meant any harm. Even for that, he still felt terribly guilty. What a heart he had! No wonder God chose him to be king.

Your deference for people will ultimately be the ladder that takes you to the summit in your field.

THE PRODUCTS OF DEFERENCE

As you already know, due to the life of consistent deference portrayed by Joseph, he was elevated to the position of Prime Minister in Egypt. He rose to the second highest position in the land, coming behind just Pharaoh, the King. You see, deference will bring you more glory than you bargained for.

The deference of David attracted the throne of the entire kingdom of Israel to him. He had wealth, power and fame. These are the things which arrogant people crave for but it keeps eluding them because of their lack of deference, first to the one who bestows all blessings (that is God) and then to their fellow men who are created in the image of God.

The disciples of Jesus deferred to him by honouring him and coming to him in private to seek reasons for their failures in their endeavours. They ended up becoming Apostles who are still relevant today, long after they've died and would be relevant all through eternity because their names are engraved on the foundations of the walls in the New Jerusalem. The one among them who was not deferent and ended up betraying his Lord lived in misery until he hung himself and he is forever excluded from the benefits of the faithful ones.

In a nutshell, be respectful, be courteous, defer to people, esteem the ideas of other people, even if they are not influential enough to take you where you intend to be, their prayers can go a long way. It was Achal Potode who said, "Never look down on anyone unless you are admiring their shoes." I believe that's a laudable principle to imbibe. As you endeavour to honour and defer to others, you will surely achieve your dreams in Jesus name.

CHAPTER 9
THE DELIGHTSOMENESS OF A WINNER

"And all nations shall call you blessed for you shall be a delightsome land saith the Lord of host."

-Malachi 3:12

PORTRAIT OF DELIGHTSOMENESS

There was once a sweet pretty lady by the name of Abigail who unfortunately was married to a man who was completely opposite to her in nature. His name was Nabal.

David got wind of a feast that Nabal was having to celebrate his prosperity, so he sent his men to Nabal asking him to give whatever he could to the men to nourish them considering the fact they had been very nice to the herders of Nabal while they tended to his flock of sheep in the fields.

Their request was greeted with an incredible rebuff. Nabal would not even give as much as a slice of bread to the itinerant men of David who desperately needed any help they could get as they were almost always on the run. He further derided David by asking the servant, "Who is David? And who is the son of Jesse? There be many servants now a days that break away every man from his master. Shall I then take my bread and my water and my flesh that I have killed for my shearers and give it unto men, who I know not whence they be" (1 Samuel 25:10, 11)?

When David heard what Nabal said, he was filled with rage. He ordered his men to get their weapons and head to Nabal's house for a total massacre. While they were on their way to Nabal's house, one of Nabal's servants informed his wife, Abigail, of what Nabal had done to provoke the ire of David.

Abigail immediately discerned that danger was imminent. She hurriedly put together many loaves of bread, wine, many other provisions and ran to accost David on the way. When she met him, she bowed before him entreating him to pardon the foolishness of her husband and refrain from shedding blood which would mar his impeccable reputation. She further offered him the provisions which she brought with her. Her delightsomeness just paralyzed David and took every bit of wind from his sail. It doesn't matter if you are a Hitler or a Napoleon, when you meet someone this nice, all your anger will dissipate in a hurry.

Of course, David accepted her gifts and decided not to go after her husband anymore because he was enthralled by her sweetness. I mean who will turn down the request of such an angelic personality? I doubt if there is any rational thinking person who would.

You see, it pays to be nice. When you are a good natured person who is just about loving people and being fun to be around, people will find you irresistible. They will gladly go out of their way to make your day. If on the other hand you are cranky, fault finding and unkind, people will always try to avoid you even in your time of need. I'm sure by now you already know how important people are for the actualization of your goals. You are not likely to win if you don't have people on your side.

PROFILING DELIGHTSOME PEOPLE

If there is one thing that delightsome people have in common, it's a smile. You can't find a delightsome person going all over the place all moody, melancholic and forlorn. They are always upbeat, optimistic and wearing a beautiful smile. A smile doesn't cost a dime, but it is more powerful than a knife for whereas a knife cuts into the body and goes no further, a smile reaches to the depth of the soul. If you can just learn to wear a beautiful smile all the time, you will be on your way to achieving great feats.

Another trait delightsome people share is their ability to stick around in times of need. The saying goes, "A friend in need is a friend indeed." Proverbs 17:17 says, "A friend loves at all times and a brother is born for adversity."

A typical example of such a delightsome acquaintance is Ruth. She had been married to one of Naomi's sons. Naomi later lost her husband and both her sons including Ruth's husband. She practically lost everything she had when she left Israel as an immigrant to Moab in search of greener pastures. When Naomi decided to return to her native land, Ruth decided she would go with her. Hard as Naomi tried to dissuade Ruth from coming with her, her words fell on deaf ears. Even though Ruth was still young and beautiful at the time and could have easily found another suitor to marry her, her love for her mother in-law made her stick with her and pledged her allegiance to follow her wherever she would go, identify with her people and serve her God. How sweet of her! Delightsome people are always available, ready to lend a hand, ready to provide a shoulder to lean on and wipe a tear. Everyone wants to have one or two of such people around them.

Furthermore, delightsome people are not easily provoked. It will take a great deal of wrong to provoke a delightsome person. They have a huge capacity to absorb a great deal of shock and maintain their strides in their journey. Can you imagine people hurling stones at you and you still have the nerve to pray that God will not lay that sin to their charge? That was precisely what Stephen did. His delightsomeness was out of this world.

Delightsome people always look on the bright side of things. They are generally positive in their outlook on life. They are optimists. They endeavour to keep hope alive, however bad the situation appears and more often than not, things turn out alright.

It's impossible to scrutinize a delightsome person without noticing their benevolent nature. They are givers by nature. They love to help people as much as they can and their generosity draws people to them and earns them the affection of people.

PROFITS OF DELIGHTSOMENESS

The delightsomeness of Abigail in the story we considered earlier didn't just spare her husband's life, it won the heart of David. The seed of her kindness sown in the heart of David kept germinating until it grew into a huge tree of love, such that after the death of her husband, David could not help asking for her hand in marriage, she said yes and the rest as they say is history. Her delightsomeness gave her access to the heart of the soon to be King and eventually made her a queen.

To live up to your billing as a congenital winner, you need to be nice and thoughtful. Malachi 3:12 says, "And all nations shall call you blessed, for you shall be a delightsome land says the Lord of host." In other words, your delightsomeness will attract the blessings of God your way. Everyone will see the blessings of God upon your life because you are pleasant, loving and caring.

In the case of Ruth, she followed her mother in-law to her native land as she pledged to do and ended up marrying a wealthy man by name Boaz. Both of them became the ancestors of Jesus Christ. So it's impossible to trace the genealogy of Jesus without talking about Ruth. How more relevant can one be? She became a heroine of faith because she was delightsome.

In John 6, we find a young boy who was kind enough to give up his five loaves and two pieces of fish to enable Christ feed the multitude who came to listen to his teachings. The boy did not consider what he would eat later; he just gave all he had to Jesus.

Jesus blessed the bread and fish, multiplied them and was able to feed 5000 men beside women and children. After everyone had eaten their fill, they still had 12 baskets full of bread and fish. I'm pretty sure that delightsome boy would not have left that place empty handed. He must have left with enough bread and fish which he could sell to earn a substantial income.

The seeds of kindness you sow will always yield a harvest of greatness. Luke 6:38 says, "Give and it shall be given unto you. Good measure, pressed down, shaken together and running over shall men give unto your bosom. For with the same measure that ye mete withal it shall be measured to you again."

When you go out of your way to help people, you attract multiple helpers your way. As you add delightsomeness to all the other virtues you've acquired since we began this journey, your winning will be much more attainable.

CHAPTER 10
THE DECORUM OF A WINNER

"A man who understands decorum and the courtesies is a great treasure. I hope to train and send into society as many such men as I can."

-Mas Oyama

UNDERSTANDING OF DECORUM

The revered Pastor E. A. Adeboye once shared an account of how he was denied the opportunity to travel abroad because of lack of basic table etiquette.

During his days at the University of Nigeria Nsukka, the University had an exchange programme with the Michigan State University, USA, which allowed them send their bright students to the USA for further learning. Before they selected the students to make the trip, they subjected them to various tests. As a distinction student, Enoch Adeboye aced all the tests.

The final test was to be carried out in the dining room. Of course, they had no idea that was part of the test. They were each served a roll of bread and a bowl of soup. He grabbed his bread, dipped it into his bowl of soup and starting munching. When the man taking note noticed his mouth was full, he asked him what he would do when he gets to America. He naturally had speech impediments because of the content of his mouth, so he couldn't answer properly.

After they had had the meal, they were served hot tea. He couldn't drink directly from the cup because the tea was quite hot, so he resorted to drinking it with his spoon. For his ignorance of basic table etiquette, he failed the test and was dropped from the list of those to make the trip to the US at the time. (19) That was many years ago, though. He later learnt those etiquettes and other etiquettes that make for a life of decorum and he has grown to be one of the most powerful men in the world.

Decorum is defined as appropriate social behaviour. That is propriety of conduct. Anyone who hopes to excel in a particular field must learn the acceptable standard behaviour in that field.

Imagine someone who gets employed in a new organization and fails to understand the values, dress code, acceptable behaviour and modus operandi of the organization. He is not likely to last long in that organization. To maximize the winning potential in you, you must endeavour to learn acceptable ways of eating, dressing, interacting and comporting yourself around people.

You don't come to a formal setting and start chatting and laughing with reckless abandon! You can't dress shabbily for an interview. You can't afford to dress for an interview as though you are going to the night club. You are most definitely going to lose that appointment. By all means dress and comport yourself in such a manner as is acceptable in whatever setting you find yourself.

I remember attending an interview without putting on a jacket. I just felt a shirt and tie would suffice. I soon discovered they couldn't suffice though because one of my interviewers specifically asked for my jacket. He wasn't happy that I didn't have one on. Thankfully, I still got the job by the grace of God but that has thought me never to go for an interview without a jacket.

MERITS OF DECORUM

Proverbs 22:11 says, "He that loveth pureness of heart, for the grace of his lips, the King shall be his friend."

What that passage is saying is that your ability to think right and act right will attract you to royalty. When you are someone who always displays decorum in all you do, you will definitely be sought for in the palace.

Daniel, Shadrach, Meshach and Abednego were full of decorum in all their dealings in Babylon so much so that you couldn't possibly fault them in anyway. Their dressing was on point, the table etiquette was flawless, and their attitude to work was top-notch. Their lives were simply impeccable. Little wonder they were the favourites of the king. They were all promoted to enviable positions. Your attention to decorum will surely catapult you to the top.

Psalm 50:23 says, "Who so offereth praise glorifieth me; and to him that orders his conversation aright will I show the salvation of God."

God is saying it is good to praise him. When you praise him, you are glorifying him and he appreciates that. However, it is to the man that orders his conversation aright that he will show his salvation. In order words, it's the man who speaks correctly, dresses correctly, and lives correctly that will see the manifestation of his saving power.

When you live a life of decorum, God comes through for you all the time and you keep winning. Some other people who violate the principles of decorum will think it is partiality. They'd wonder why you are the only one forging ahead and winning all the time. The answer is in what God has said in very clear terms. The man who orders his conversation aright will always experience his salvation.

There was an established protocol for offering sacrifice in Israel. Nobody was qualified to do it apart from the priest ordained by God. Out of impatience, Saul went ahead to offer sacrifice because he had to go for battle and Samuel who was ordained to make the sacrifice was taking too long to show up. Because of that inability to maintain decorum, he was rejected as king and David who lived a life of decorum was appointed in his place. Even though you are a congenital winner, lack of decorum will repress your winning potential and cost you your place in destiny.

You will do yourself a whole lot of good to learn what is acceptable in the field of your endeavour and adhere strictly to them. Your resultant decorum will take you places to the glory of God.

CHAPTER 11
THE DOMINION OF A WINNER

"Authority is ability to rule.
Dominion is rulership."

–Sherry K. White

Dominion is the ability to exercise power or sovereignty over something or someone.

In order to make your winning potential a reality, you must exercise dominion over certain things. If you are defeated or under the power of these things, you will be incapacitated and your winning potential will remain dormant. In this chapter, we will be exploring these things which must of necessity come under your dominion in order for you to be the winner you were born to be.

THE WINNER'S DOMINION OVER SIN

Most folks do not like to accept it, but sin is a major limiting factor preventing people from becoming the winners they were created to be. What is sin? Sin is violating God's laws.

God's laws are essentially moral and are intended to prevent us from self-harm and hurting others. When we intentionally violate God's laws, we suffer great repercussions which significantly impede our progress in our journey towards fulfilment.

Countless teenagers are in prison today who once had very promising futures but now wallow in regret as they consider the pieces of their shattered dreams. They landed there because of sin.

Many teenage girls who could have made intelligent journalists, company directors, exceptional authors, and so on are regretting the choices they made as they lie in the bed of affliction brought upon them by several sexually transmitted diseases, seeing nothing but the ashes of their once glorious destinies.

Politicians have been humiliated and impeached due to corrupt practices and immoral behaviour. Highly promising lives have been confined to oblivion because of some heinous crime. When God tells us to stay away from sin, it is because he knows sin can only hurt us and dim the light of his glory invested in us at creation.

It is therefore imperative that anyone who hopes to be an enduring winner achieves dominion over sin. How does that happen?

Romans 6:14 says, "And sin shall not have dominion over you for you are not under the law but under grace." If we apply the law of non-contradiction which states that contradictory propositions cannot both be true in the same sense at the same time, then we recognize the error of those who claim we cannot have dominion over sin as long as we are in this world. God's word says sin shall not have dominion over us when we come under his grace. The direct corollary of that statement is that we shall have dominion over sin as long as we are under God's grace. How then do we come under God's grace?

Grace is actually a personality. Jesus is the personification of grace. So when a man identifies with Jesus he comes in contact with grace and comes under the influence of grace.

John 1:14 tells us, "And the Word (Jesus) was made flesh and dwelt among us and we beheld his glory, the glory as of the only begotten of the Father, full of GRACE and TRUTH" (Emphasis mine).

So, you see, Jesus is the expression and embodiment of grace. In order to come under the grace of God therefore, one must turn away from his sins and accept Jesus Christ as his Lord and Saviour.

Acts 2:38 says, "Then Peter said unto them, Repent and be baptized every one of you in the name of Jesus Christ for the remission (removal, absolution and elimination) of sins, and ye shall receive the gift of the Holy Ghost" (Amplification mine).

It is abundantly clear therefore that when we come to Jesus in repentance from our sins and accept his vicarious sacrifice for the remission of our sins, we receive freedom not just from the guilt of sin, but also from the power of sin. What is the effect of God's grace in our lives?

Titus 2:11-12 says, "For the grace of God that brings salvation has appeared unto all men, teaching us that denying ungodliness and worldly lusts, we should live soberly, righteously and godly in this present world."

You see, my dear friend, you can live righteously in this present world by the help of God's grace. You do not have to wait until you get to heaven to be righteous. You can exercise dominion over sin right here, right now. That's what Jesus died on the cross to achieve. He couldn't have been short-changed. He came to save you from your sins, so thus liberated from every limiting factor you can spread your wings and fly to the peak of life. Open up your life to the power of His grace right now and you will never know another defeat in your life.

The major battle reside in your mind. If you think you can have **dominion** over sin you certainly will. If you however think you cannot have dominion over sin, you will remain a perpetual slave to sin and never be able to achieve your dreams. That's the reason why we are counselled in Romans 6:11 to "reckon ourselves to be dead indeed unto sins but alive unto God through Jesus Christ our Lord." When you are dead to something you no longer know of its existence. When you are dead to something you are unresponsive to it. It has no influence upon you anymore.

That should be our mental disposition towards sin. *I am dead to sin and alive to God through Jesus Christ, therefore sin has no place in my life.* If you continue to think that way, sin will disappear from your life because "as a man thinks in his heart so is he" (Proverbs 23:7).You eventually become exactly like your predominant thoughts.

I welcome you to a life of dominion over sin and I assure you of more wins than you ever imagined as you explore this life.

THE WINNER'S DOMINION OVER SICKNESS

Sickness can be a major limiting factor on the way of people trying to achieve their life goals. The life of many people who would have been really glorious and impactful have been unfortunately cut short by certain diseases. Some who managed to survive are left with lifelong complications.

As a matter of fact, a detailed discussion of disease causation is beyond the scope of this book but suffice it to say that there is a fine interplay between genetic makeup and environmental factors in the aetiology of most diseases. The literacy level, social standing and health seeking behaviour of people also impact significantly on their exposure to diseases and overall health status.

To prevent the limitation that comes with disease, a winner must be armed with necessary health education to help prevent the preventable diseases. Prevention, they say, is better than cure. Adherence to proper hygiene practices such as regular hand washing, drinking of uncontaminated water and eating properly cooked food prepared under utmost sanitary conditions will go a long way in preventing quite a number of diseases.

Brushing your teeth regularly, having a proper bath at least twice in a day, and keeping away from mosquitoes by using insecticide treated nets or indoor residual spraying of insecticides will go a long way in keeping you healthy.

The need for proper diet and regular exercise cannot be overemphasized. You need to eat smart and live smart in order to be your best at all times. Indiscriminate eating coupled with lack of adequate exercise will make you add so much weight and become obese.

Obesity will in turn attract diabetes, hypertension, heart disease, stroke, osteoarthritis, fatty liver disease and even some form of cancer. It will definitely be in your best interest to avoid all these diseases by eating smart and exercising regularly.

The next important factor in keeping sicknesses at bay would be routine hospital visitation for general health appraisal. From time to time you should go see your doctor to examine you and do some basic tests so as to tell your general state of health and expose any insipient health challenge.

You should also endeavour to take your medications as prescribed by your doctor when he finds a disease needing treatment. Do not skip doses or discontinue the medication once you feel a bit better. If you do, you are asking for a more severe form of that illness which is not likely to respond to the drugs that you have abused. You should also avoid the use of herbal concoctions. They pose significant risk to your liver. By all means stay with orthodox care.

Above all, you should trust the Lord God to keep you in health and heal you if for any reason you fall sick. He said "I am the Lord that healeth thee" (Exodus 15:26).

You should also take advantage of the stripes that Jesus bore for the purpose of our healings. 1 Peter 2:24 says, "Who his own self bear our sins in his own body on the tree, that we being dead to sins, should live unto righteousness: by whose stripes ye were healed."

Therefore, for those in Christ Jesus, our healing is a sealed deal. It was accomplished by Christ on the cross. We can claim it and enjoy uninterrupted health while being the winners we were born to be.

THE WINNER'S DOMINION OVER SATAN

Before I wrap up this chapter, I will like to address the final threat to the manifestation of your winning potential. He is Satan. He doesn't mean well for anyone and he will stop at nothing in his bid to ruin your life. Jesus rightly described him when he said, "The thief comes not but for to steal and to kill and to destroy: I am come that they might have life and that they might have it more abundantly."

You see that's precisely the goal of the devil: to steal from you, kill you and ultimately destroy you. He has destroyed the lives of many great men who did not know how to exercise dominion over him. You will do well to learn how to put him where he belongs or take him for granted at your own peril.

My mother once shared an experience she had while she was pregnant with me. She was returning from a church program one evening with my elder sister strapped to her back and was heavy with me in her womb.

Suddenly she saw a scary monster in human form with terrible looking claws advancing towards her and asking her, "Who told you to conceive?"

Before my mum could recover from the shock of seeing such a grotesque personality talking to her, the personality just lifted its claws and started advancing them towards my mother's womb in an attempt to tear me out. My mother immediately screamed "the blood of Jesus!" That was how the personality froze there and couldn't advance its claws any further.

Then the personality took a closer look at my mum and started screaming "What kind of person is this?"

Only God knows exactly what he saw that made him so scared. He eventually turned and ran away as fast as it could. It wasn't a dream, a trance or hallucination. It was a real experience.

You see, the devil knew the child in my mother's womb was going to be a winner and would also help many people recognize that they are congenital winners thus making them unbeatable winners, so he wanted to destroy me before I even stepped foot in the world. However, he was frustrated because my mother had dominion over him. She exercised her dominion over him by the grace of God and he fled away. That's why I am here today!

Everyone who comes into the family of God through faith in the Lord Jesus Christ receives authority over the devil. That we all have that authority is one thing; whether or not we exercise it is another thing.

In Luke10:19, Jesus said, "Behold I give unto you power to tread on serpents and scorpions and over all the power of the enemy and nothing shall by any means hurt you." What assurance of victory can be more than that? Unfortunately, even though we have been given authority over the Devil, many people do not exercise it and thus do not enjoy dominion over the devil.

A policeman has the authority of the state to apprehend and detain criminals. If he is ignorant of that authority or chooses to look the other way when he sees crime being perpetrated, that authority will only remain dormant but not exercised. Same applies to believers. If you do not recognize that Christ has given you power over the works of the enemy and you keep wailing and crying about the activities of the devil, you will keep being a victim of his antics.

Revelation 12:11 says, "They overcame him by the blood of the Lamb and by the word of their testimony." That is precisely how to overcome the devil. You invoke the power in the blood of Jesus and testify of God's mighty works in scriptures and in your life. The devil will never be able to stand before you. Whether in the day or in the night, the skilful use of the twin weapon of the blood of Jesus and the words of our testimony will surely give the devil a technical knockout.

As you begin to exercise dominion over the devil, nothing and no one will stop you from becoming the Winner you were born to be.

CHAPTER 12
THE DESTINATION OF A WINNER

"Success is a journey, not a destination. The doing is often more important than the outcome."

-Arthur Ashe

In the concluding chapter of this book I'd like to make you appreciate the fact that there is more to life than winning in our endeavours. Success is not necessarily our destination. After you have won all the laurels and bagged all the degrees and received all the awards, what next? Is that all there is to life or is there more?

The successes we win in life are not ends in themselves; they are means to an end. The ultimate end is making it to the kingdom of God at the end of our lives. That is in fact the real victory because the real battle of the enemy is not necessarily to make you a failure in life but to damn your soul in hell fire. If you win all the laurels and get all the accolades in life and fail to make it to heaven, you would have failed the most crucial exam.

The destination of those who win in life and win in death is heaven. What does it take to get there?

Requirements For Reaching The Winner's Destination

Psalm 15:1 gives us a fairly precise answer: "Lord, who shall abide in thy tabernacle? Who shall dwell in thy holy hill?"

The response promptly followed in verses 2-5:

> *"He that walketh uprightly and worketh righteousness and speaketh the truth in his heart. He that backbiteth not with his tongue nor doeth evil to his neighbour, nor taketh up a reproach against his neighbour. In whose eyes a vile person is contemned, but he honours them that fear the Lord. He that sweareth to his own hurt and changeth not. He that putteth not out his money to usury nor taketh reward against the innocent. He that doeth these things shall never be moved."*

Wow! That is a long list of requirements for getting to the kingdom of God. It is however impossible to do all of those things by our own strength, which is why God sent Jesus to die for our sins on the cross of Calvary so that we can be partakers of His righteousness by faith.

2 Corinthians 5:21 says, "For he hath made him to be sin for us who knew no sin, that we might be made the righteousness of God in him."

Faith in the Lord Jesus Christ imparts Gods righteousness to our lives which enables us live to please Him in all we do thus making us winners in life and winners in death, headed for the destination of all true winners which is heaven.

Readiness For That Imminent Transition

Even if we live to be a thousand years in this world, we will definitely have to leave this world someday. There is no doubt about that. I feel that reality should be sobering enough to make every one of us prepare for our eternal destination.

Jesus Christ Himself told us over and over to watch and be careful because we cannot tell exactly when he will return. In Matthew 25, He told the parable of the 10 virgins, out of whom 5 were wise and the others foolish. The wise virgins had sufficient oil in their lamps. In other words they were consistently watching and hoping for the return of the master. The foolish virgins were laissez faire, indifferent and unconcerned. They never saw the need to get sufficient oil in their lamps in readiness for the master's return. Unfortunately for them, the master came before they had the chance to wake up from their state of spiritual slumber and they were shut out of his Kingdom.

Like my beloved Pastor W. F. Kumuyi will always emphasize, "Without Holiness no man shall see the Lord," heaven is a prepared place for prepared saints. No one will get there by chance. It takes a life of consistent holiness enabled by the grace of God through faith in Christ to get to heaven. A life of sin will most definitely deny you entrance to the kingdom of God because God is of purer eyes than to behold sin (Habakkuk 1:13).

We all have the responsibility to prepare to meet our Creator. We will surely stand before Him to give account of the life we have lived. What will you tell Him on that day?

Hebrews 9:27 says, "And as it is appointed unto men once to die but after this the judgment."

When you stand before the cross examination of the God of all the earth, who has perfect knowledge of all the details of your life from the time of your conception to the time of your death, will the verdict be in your favour? Will you win that examination? That is the winning that matters the most. That is the victory that gives you a place in God's heavenly kingdom.

If you draw your last breath this moment and drop dead, where will you spend eternity? Will you be in heaven or in hell?

Revelation 21;8 says, "But the fearful and unbelieving and the abominable and murderers and whoremongers and sorcerers and idolaters and all liars shall have their part in the lake which burneth with fire and brimstone which is the second death."

If you are not sure of making heaven should you die now, you can bow your head and pray to God this moment. Ask him to forgive you all your sins and invite Jesus into your life to be your Lord and Saviour.

Quietly pray this prayer from the depth of your heart:

Lord Jesus, I come to you today

I acknowledge the fact that I am a sinner and worthy of your judgment

I ask you to forgive me all my sins and help me never to return to them

I believe you died on the cross to save me from my sins

I now accept you as my Lord and Saviour and promise to serve you until the end of my life.

Thank you for saving my soul. In Jesus name!

Now you are absolutely ready to win all through life and win in eternity. What a trip this has been! I look forward to celebrating your success stories. Do well to keep in touch as these trophies begin to roll in. Thank you for taking your time to read through this book. God bless you abundantly. Be assured of my deepest love and highest regards. Cheers!

THE END

REFERENCES

1. https://www.dailymail.co.uk/sport/football/arti   icle-6158781/Carlos-Teves-opens-Lionel-Messi-cristiano-Ronaldos-training-ground-routine.html

2   https://www.marca.com/en/football/internationaln-football/2018/06/19/5b28d4d0468aeb09588b458b.html

3. Gifted hands by Ben Carson

4.https://en.m.wikipedia.org/wiki/Emancipation_Proclam mation

5.https://www.cartierwomensinitiative.com/canfidate/lur na-rutto

6.https://www.nobelprize.org/prizes/peace/1993/press-release/

7.https://en.m.wikipedia.org/wiki/Anthony_Joshua_vs._And y_Ruiz_Jr.

8.https://www.aa.com.tr/en/sports/boxing-joshua-beats-ruiz-to-reclaim-heavyweight-title/1667191

9. https://en.m.wikipedia.org/wiki/Mount_Everest

10. https://en.m.wikipedia.org/wiki/Lionel_Messi

11. https://en.m.wikipedia.org/wiki/I_Have_a_Dream

12. http://www.analytictech.com/mb021/mlk.html

13. Page 68, My Transition Hours by Dr Goodluck Ebele Jonathan

14.https://en.m.wikipedia.org/wiki/Goodluck_Jonathan#cite_note-96

15.https://www.dailytrust.com.ng/un-appointment-jonathans-legacy-of-peace-speaking-for-him-frank.html

16.https://en.m.wikipedia.org/wiki/Nick_Vujicic

17.https://www.vanguardngr.com/2019/09/our-evacuation-of-nigerians-may-end-xenophobia-attacks-in-south-africa-allen-onyema/

18.https://www.theguardian.com/sport/2009/apr/11/usain-bolt-athletics-interview-records-100m

19.https://www.nairaland.com/5120808/failed-critical-examination-pastor-E.A.Adeboye

ABOUT THE AUTHOR

Francis Ojima is a Medical Doctor, Music Minister and Public Speaker who is passionate about helping young people discover and maximize their God-given potentials. As one who has tasted first hand of the infinite capabilities of the grace of God at work in man, he seeks to help as many as possible discover and walk in the riches of that grace.

He is currently undergoing his residency training in the Surgery Department of Federal Medical Centre, Lokoja. Francis is married to Joy and they both reside in Lokoja, Kogi State, Nigeria.